PREFACE TO POETRY

Robert Hawkins

Preface to POETRY

BASIC BOOKS, INC., PUBLISHERS

NEW YORK   LONDON

THIRD PRINTING

© 1965 by Robert Hawkins

Library of Congress Catalog Card Number 65–25238
Manufactured in the United States of America
Designed by Jacqueline Schuman

For **D. J.,** who read me my first poem

Preface

The twenty-five poems in this anthology are an arbitrary selection intended to provide the reader with a "laboratory" in which the poetic process may be examined. And, since this book is intended to be an introduction to poetry as a whole rather than to a particular genre or to the works of a certain period, the poems discussed, although diverse in nature, are for the most part well known.

To avoid the confusion likely when a beginner is confronted with a mass of widely differing poetry, the number of works chosen has been deliberately limited. By concentrating on a few poems, the newcomer to verse may attain a sense of depth as well as breadth.

The commentaries emphasize some of the mechanics of verse, which the author regards as essential to an understanding of meaning as well as to an appreciation of lyric beauty. For practical assistance, a note on meter has been included, together with a glossary of terms useful in analysis. Also included are brief biographies of the poets represented and an index of authors, titles, and first lines.

Lakeville, Connecticut   Robert Hawkins
August 1965

Acknowledgments

I must acknowledge, first of all, my indebtedness to my editor, Patricia Lowe Pitzele, for her good nature and hard work during the preparation of this book. Sincerest thanks are due also to my colleagues, Richard Crocker Gurney and John G. Bowen, for their learned help; to the Reverend James W. Hyde, Margaret Barry Beaumont, and my co-worker on other volumes, Denise Restout, for their excellent suggestions; to Anna Walters, who cheerfully deciphered and typed the manuscript; and to the Trustees of the Hotchkiss School, who on the recommendation of the headmaster, Albert W. Olsen, Jr., sponsored a portion of this project.

Finally, I must express my gratitude to the countless Hotchkiss boys who, year after year, have guided and stimulated my teaching of poetic appreciation.

Contents

3

4

5

6

PREFACE TO POETRY

Introduction

Most of us have very little time for poetry in the twenty-four hours that make up our day. If we think about poetry at all, we may feel in a vague way that we should consider more about it. But somehow there is always a game or a television program or some other distraction to occupy us that is seemingly of far greater excitement than strings of words on a page. Perhaps a good story in a book or a magazine may tempt us, but not poetry.

It is hard to become interested, I know, in words that are presented in a form that differs so greatly from that of our regular reading matter. In themselves, the words may be difficult or even meaningless to us; they often seem to have little to do with real life. Yet, whatever the reason, we do find poetry hard to enjoy; there are easier ways of amusing ourselves. We read poetry when we have to, when it is assigned for homework; and we find it a chore.

Poetry, like sport, cannot be enjoyed without personal involvement and knowledge. Suppose, for example, you were to watch a football game for the first time, and had never played the game. Much of it would seem to be pretty mysterious. But when you have watched a few games, learned some of the rules, and become accustomed to the patterns made by the movements of players on the field or the flight of the ball, it begins to make sense. It becomes interesting, even exciting, to watch. And so it is with poetry. Once the pattern of the words on the page becomes less strange to us, gradually those words can start to excite us.

Poetry is, of course, more than a game and more than pattern. Besides, the writing and reading of it are universal experiences. Since early history man has conveyed his deepest and most treasured thoughts in the form of verse. Poetic description enables us to share events, thoughts, or feelings that we may have experienced for ourselves, yet have not managed to express in words.

A poet sees and describes things from a highly individual viewpoint. His special eye and understanding set him apart, and he has the power to illuminate a scene, an emotion, or a thought in a way that we are not able to achieve for ourselves. His writing broadens our awareness and enriches our experience.

At the end of this collection is T. S. Eliot's "Journey of the Magi." We are familiar with the story it tells; we have sung of it in carols and acted it out in Christmas pageants. But when we read this poem, we become part of it; suddenly we are there, outdoors in the cold. We share the uncomfortable, dirty business of traveling by camel. And the religious significance of the story in all its poignancy comes home to us as never before; we are able to identify ourselves with the Wise Men, to feel their weariness, their uncertainty, and a little of their wonder. This is made possible by the poet's art.

Although poetry is not read aloud much today, it remains, nonetheless, an oral art; it is meant to be heard. The best way to enjoy poetry is, therefore, to hear it read or to read it aloud carefully. Pronouncing each word accurately, while neither adding nor overlooking words, is essential. The changing of one syllable can disrupt the rhythm of an entire line and even alter its character.

One must live with a poem for a while before it becomes

significant; and the best way to live with a poem is to memorize it. Try it for yourself. If what you have chosen is long, such as *The Ancient Mariner* or *Sohrab and Rustum*, then commit to memory those portions that especially appeal to you. Ask yourself why you chose a particular passage, for the more you know about a poem the more likely you are to appreciate it. Your answer will help your enjoyment of poetry in general; it may even encourage you to read other works by the same author.

It is very easy to memorize verse, although you probably do not think so. Whatever you choose, whether it be an entire poem or a brief passage, make sure that you understand all the words (use the dictionary). Try to feel the rhythm; tap it out if you like. Primarily, rhyme is intended to please the ear, but it is also one of the best devices to aid one's memory. Once you have been through the entire poem, read it again aloud. Then try to recite it without looking at the printed page. After repeating this process several times, write out the poem from memory. Correct your written version against the text. It should not be necessary to repeat this last step more than once. But, above all, try to memorize a poem or a poetic passage as a unit, not line by line.

I

Popular and Literary Ballads

The ballad may be classified as either "popular" or "literary." If it is popular, the ballad evolved from a folk poem—that is, it has been transmitted anonymously by word of mouth and, in the process, has undergone various changes, so that several versions of the same ballad may exist. If a ballad is termed *literary*, this means that it has been written comparatively recently by a known author in the style of the popular ballad—for example, *The Rime of the Ancient Mariner* (pp. 10–33) and "Danny Deever" (pp. 38–39). Even today the tradition of the popular ballad is not dead. A national or world-shaking event will often prompt its composition. Conspicuous examples are the Calypso songs of the West Indies (pp. 40–41).

Many of the popular ballads have their origins in a rough, primitive society and are, therefore, concerned with the sterner human realities of life—death, intrigue, treachery, infidelity, to name but a few. The popular ballad is in its language fresh, lively, and vigorous. It would be unfair to invite close comparison with the polished elegance of later poetical works; but coming early in our literary history, ballads provide a good beginning for the study of poetry. There are today hundreds of popular ballads to choose from; those included here are well known and typical of their kind.

The most productive period of balladry occurred between the thirteenth and fifteenth centuries along the borders of England and Scotland. In those days ballads were usually sung, or chanted. Let us imagine a large baronial hall where lords and ladies, squires and henchmen, are gathered to eat and relax. On a balcony overlooking the hall sits an itinerant bard, there to entertain them with his ballads; occasionally he plucks at his eight-stringed harp to maintain pitch. The sound the minstrel makes with this instrument we would find strange, for it is totally unlike the fuller and involved harmonies to which these same ballads are set today. The countless phonograph recordings now on the market are pleasant to hear, but there is no doubt that their presentation bears little resemblance to the form in which ballads were originally heard.

To be enjoyed ballads need not, however, be set to music. Today we most often hear them spoken or read them in books— they are printed as a rule in the language of the age, not unlike the Lowlands speech of modern Scotland. Because they were intended to be heard and not read, ballads are easy to understand; they do not demand the detailed study required by more elaborate works.

In the ballad, each stanza paints a little scene in careful detail. The figurative language and complicated imagery of later English poetry is rarely found in these narratives. The description is clear, whereas interpretation is left to the reader. There is, none-theless, much that is subtle and suggestive in these ballads, which explains why they withstand frequent repetition. The balladeer seems to have been reluctant to express himself bluntly. You may have learned for yourself that suggestion is sometimes stronger than direct statement. Suggestion has a way of working stealthily into your awareness. It has, also, the quality of a puzzle, a puzzle that you can only solve for yourself, in your own way.

The ballad that follows is one of the most familiar.

The Twa Corbies

As I was walking all alane
I heard twa corbies making a mane:
The tane unto the tither did say,
"Whar sall we gang and dine the day?"

"—In behint yon auld fail dyke
I wot there lies a new-slain knight;
And naebody kens that he lies there
But his hawk, his hound, and his lady fair.

"His hound is to the hunting gane,
His hawk to fetch the wild-fowl hame,
His lady's ta'en another mate,
So we may mak our dinner sweet.

"Ye'll sit on his white hause–bane,
And I'll pike out his bonny blue e'en:
Wi' ae lock o' his gowden hair
We'll theek our nest when it grows bare.

"Mony a one for him maks mane,
But nane sall ken whar he is gane:
O'er his white banes, when they are bare,
The wind sall blaw for evermair."

corbies, ravens   _fail_, turf   _hause_, neck   _theek_, thatch

This ballad provides a good example of the use of suggestion, for nowhere do we find a direct statement of the wife's treachery; yet there is no doubt she arranged to have her husband murdered so that she would be free to marry another man. That the "new-slain knight" is much admired and a man of character and handsome appearance is implied, but never said outright. We are moved by his plight; yet the story is told with complete objectivity, as though the ravens could not care less about what we feel. They are, after all, interested only in a good meal and materials for their nest.

Talking birds were no more common in the Dark Ages—when this ballad became popular—than they are now, although people were once less skeptical than we are. Sinister birds that they are, these two add just the right touch for creating the mood, or atmosphere, of the poem. The final stanza of "The Twa Corbies" reaffirms the melancholy established by the second.

Another ballad, "Edward, Edward," also anonymous, is a sorrowful narrative about the blackest kind of treachery:

Edward, Edward

"Why dois your brand sae drap wi' bluid,
    Edward, Edward?
Why dois your brand sae drap wi' bluid,
    And why sae sad gang yee, O?"
"O I hae killed my hauke sae guid,
    Mither, mither;
O I hae killed my hauke sae guid,
    And I had nae mair bot hee, O."

"Your haukis bluid was nevir sae reid,
    Edward, Edward;
Your haukis bluid was nevir sae reid,
    My deir son, I tell thee, O."
O I hae killed my reid-roan steid,
    Mither, mither;
That erst was sae fair and frie, O."

sae, so   *drap,* drop   *bluid,* blood   *gang,* go   *mair,* more   *reid*
red

"Your steid was auld, and ye hae got mair,
        Edward, Edward;
Your steid was auld, and ye hae got mair;
        Sum other dule ye drie, O."
"O I hae killed my fadir deir,
        Mither, mither;
        Alas, and wae is mee, O!"

"And whatten penance wul ye drie for that,
        Edward, Edward?
And whatten penance will ye drie for that?
        My deir son, now tell me, O."
"Ile set my feit in younder boat,
        Mither, mither;
Ile set my feit in yonder boat,
        And Ile fare ovir the sea, O."

"And what wul ye doe wi' your towirs and your ha',
        Edward, Edward?
And what wul ye doe wi your towirs and your ha',
        That were sae fair to see, O?"
"Ile let thame stand tul they doun fa',
        Mither, mither;
Ile let thame stand tul they doun fa',
        For here nevir mair maun I bee, O."

"And what wul ye leive to your bairns and your wife,
        Edward, Edward?
And what wull ye leive to your bairns and your wife,
        Whan ye gang ovir the sea, O?"
"The warldis room; late them beg thrae life,
        Mither, mither;
The warldis room, late them beg thrae life,
        For thame nevir mair wul I see, O."

dule ye dree, grief you suffer   *fadir*, father   *ha'*, hall   *fa'*, fall
maun, must   *bairns*, children   *thrae*, through

"And what wul ye leive to your ain mither deir,
Edward, Edward?
And what wul ye leive to your ain mither deir,
My deir son, now tell me, O?"
"The curse of hell frae me sall ye beir,
Mither, mither,
The curse of hell frae me sall ye beir:
Sic counseils ye gave to me, O!"

sic, such

Again it is suggestion that is the powerful force in this ballad. The mother's artful questioning leads to a dramatic climax, and we are hardly aware that what actually happened is never explicitly stated. We can only surmise what counsel the mother gave her son, but we do not doubt she urged him to kill his father.

Verse Forms

It is essential to understand the meaning of the word "form" as it is applied to verse. In the type of writing we are now studying it involves meter, and rhyme, and the number of lines in a stanza. Most ballads follow pretty much the same pattern—a four-line stanza, or quatrain, of alternating iambic tetrameter and iambic trimeter, rhyming *a b c b,* although the version of "The Twa Corbies" just given is in four-line stanzas of iambic tetrameter, sometimes called long measure.

"Edward, Edward" presents several variations. In this ballad the "O" at the end of some lines gives an eerie and dramatic effect. and it also helps fill out the line metrically. Read aloud, the "O" suggests a wail. And in "Edward, Edward" we find a device frequently employed by the balladeer: repetition with a slight variation (incremental repetition). This advances the narrative slowly and builds suspense.

As you progress in your study of poetry, you will hear more and more frequently the phrase "levels of meaning." There are many such terms used in the analysis of poetry, and *The Rime of the Ancient Mariner*, a literary ballad by Samuel Taylor Coleridge (1772–1834), provides a good "laboratory" for studying them. Of course, not all poems suggest or indeed contain more than one level of meaning. But if a poem lends itself to imaginative interpretation, it increases our interest; it is important, however, that in the attempt to interpret one does not resort to guesswork.

The Rime of the Ancient Mariner

IN SEVEN PARTS

Argument

How a ship having passed the Line was driven by storms to the cold Country towards the South Pole; and how from thence she made her course to the tropical Latitude of the Great Pacific Ocean; and of the strange things that befell; and in what manner the Ancyent Marinere came back to his own Country.

PART I

An ancient Mariner meeteth three Gallants bidden to a wedding-feast and detaineth one.

It is an ancient Mariner,
And he stoppeth one of three.
"By thy long grey beard and glittering eye,
Now wherefore stopp'st thou me?

"The Bridegroom's doors are opened wide,
And I am next of kin;
The guests are met, the feast is set:
May'st hear the merry din."

He holds him with his skinny hand,
"There was a ship," quoth he.
"Hold off! unhand me, grey-beard loon!"
Eftsoons his hand dropt he.

He holds him with his glittering eye—
The Wedding-Guest stood still,
And listens like a three years' child:
The Mariner hath his will.

The Wedding-Guest sat on a stone:
He cannot choose but hear;
And thus spake on that ancient man,
The bright-eyed Mariner.

"The ship was cheered, the harbour cleared,
Merrily did we drop
Below the kirk, below the hill,
Below the lighthouse top.

"The sun came up upon the left,
Out of the sea came he!
And he shone bright, and on the right
Went down into the sea.

"Higher and higher every day,
Till over the mast at noon—"
The Wedding-Guest here beat his breast,
For he heard the loud bassoon.

The bride had paced into the hall,
Red as a rose is she;
Nodding their heads before her goes
The merry minstrelsy.

The Wedding-Guest he beat his breast,
Yet he cannot choose but hear;
And thus spake on that ancient man,
The bright-eyed Mariner.

The Wedding-Guest is spellbound by the eye of the old seafaring man, and constrained to hear his tale.

The Mariner tells how the ship sailed southward with a good wind and fair weather, till it reached the line.

The Wedding-Guest heareth the bridal music; but the Mariner continueth his tale.

The ship driven by a storm toward the south pole.

"And now the Storm-blast came, and he
Was tyrannous and strong:
He struck with his o'ertaking wings,
And chased us south along.

"With sloping masts and dripping prow,
As who pursued with yell and blow
Still treads the shadow of his foe,
And forward bends his head,
The ship drove fast, loud roared the blast,
And southward aye we fled.

"And now there came both mist and snow,
And it grew wondrous cold:
And ice, mast-high, came floating by,
As green as emerald.

The land of ice, and of fearful sounds where no living thing was to be seen.

"And through the drifts the snowy clifts
Did send a dismal sheen:
Nor shapes of men nor beasts we ken—
The ice was all between.

"The ice was here, the ice was there,
The ice was all around:
It cracked and growled, and roared and howled,
Like noises in a swound!

Till a great seabird, called the Albatross, came through the snow-fog, and was received with great joy and hospitality.

"At length did cross an Albatross,
Thorough the fog it came;
As if it had been a Christian soul,
We hailed it in God's name.

"It ate the food it ne'er had eat,
And round and round it flew.
The ice did split with a thunder-fit;
The helmsman steered us through!

"And a good south wind sprung up behind;
The Albatross did follow,
And every day, for food or play,
Came to the Mariners' hollo!

And lo! the Albatross proved a bird of good omen, and followeth the ship as it returned northward through fog and floating ice.

"In mist or cloud, on mast or shroud,
It perched for vespers nine;
Whiles all the night, through fog-smoke white,
Glimmered the white moon-shine."

"God save thee, ancient Mariner!
From the fiends, that plague thee thus!—
Why look'st thou so?"—"With my cross-bow
I shot the Albatross."

The ancient Mariner inhospitably killeth the pious bird of good omen.

PART II

"The Sun now rose upon the right;
Out of the sea came he,
Still hid in mist, and on the left
Went down into the sea.

"And the good south wind still blew behind,
But no sweet bird did follow,
Nor any day for food or play
Came to the mariners' hollo!

His shipmates
cry out
against the an-
cient Mariner,
for killing the
bird of good
luck.

"And I had done a hellish thing,
And it would work 'em woe:
For all averred, I had killed the bird
That made the breeze to blow.
'Ah wretch!' said they, 'the bird to slay,
That made the breeze to blow!'

But when the
fog cleared
off, they
justify the
same, and
thus make
themselves
accomplices
in the crime.

"Nor dim nor red, like God's own head,
The glorious Sun uprist:
Then all averred, I had killed the bird
That brought the fog and mist.
"Twas right,' said they, 'such birds to slay,
That bring the fog and mist.'

The fair
breeze con-
tinues; the
ship enters the
Pacific Ocean,
and sails
northward,
even till it
reaches the
line.

"The fair breeze blew, the white foam flew,
The furrow followed free;
We were the first that ever burst
Into that silent sea.

The ship hath
been suddenly
becalmed.

"Down dropt the breeze, the sails dropt down,
'Twas sad as sad could be;
And we did speak only to break
The silence of the sea!

"All in a hot and copper sky,
The bloody Sun, at noon,
Right up above the mast did stand,
No bigger than the Moon.

"Day after day, day after day,
We stuck, nor breath nor motion;
As idle as a painted ship
Upon a painted ocean.

"Water, water, everywhere,
And all the boards did shrink;
Water, water, everywhere
Nor any drop to drink.

And the Albatross begins to be avenged.

"The very deep did rot: O Christ!
That ever this should be!
Yea, slimy things did crawl with legs
Upon the slimy sea.

A spirit had followed them; one of the invisible inhabitants of this planet, neither departed souls nor angels; concerning whom the learned Jew, Josephus, and the Platonic Constantinopolitan, Michael

"About, about, in reel and rout
The death-fires danced at night;
The water, like a witch's oils,
Burnt green, and blue, and white.

"And some in dreams assurèd were
Of the Spirit that plagued us so;
Nine fathom deep he had followed us
From the land of mist and snow.

Psellus, may be consulted. They are very numerous, and there is no climate or element without one or more.

"And every tongue, through utter drought,
Was withered at the root;
We could not speak, no more than if
We had been choked with soot.

The shipmates, in their sore distress would fain throw the whole guilt on the ancient Mariner: in sign whereof they hang the dead sea-bird round his neck.

"Ah! well-a-day! what evil looks
Had I from old and young!
Instead of the cross, the Albatross
About my neck was hung."

PART III

"There passed a weary time. Each throat
Was parched, and glazed each eye.

A weary time! a weary time!
How glazed each weary eye,
When, looking westward, I beheld
A something in the sky.

"At first it seemed a little speck,
And then it seemed a mist;
It moved and moved, and took at last
A certain shape, I wist.

"A speck, a mist, a shape, I wist!
And still it neared and neared:
As if it dodged a water sprite,
It plunged and tacked and veered.

"With throats unslaked, with black lips baked,
We could nor laugh nor wail;
Through utter drought all dumb we stood!
I bit my arm, I sucked the blood,
And cried, 'A sail! a sail!'

"With throats unslaked, with black lips baked,
Agape they hear me call:

Gramercy! they for joy did grin,
And all at once their breath drew in,
As they were drinking all.

" 'See! see!' (I cried) 'she tacks no more!
Hither to work us weal;
Without a breeze, without a tide,
She steadies with upright keel!'

"The western wave was all a-flame,
The day was well-nigh done!
Almost upon the western wave
Rested the broad bright Sun;
When that strange shape drove suddenly
Betwixt us and the Sun.

"And straight the Sun was flecked with bars,
(Heaven's Mother send us grace!)
As if through a dungeon-grate he peered
With broad and burning face.

It seemeth him but the skeleton of a ship.

" 'Alas!' (thought I, and my heart beat loud)
'How fast she nears and nears!
Are those her sails that glance in the sun,
Like restless gossameres?

" 'Are those her ribs through which the sun
Did peer, as through a grate?
And is that woman all her crew?
Is that a Death? and are there two?
Is Death that woman's mate?'

And its ribs are seen as bars on the face of the setting Sun. The Spectre-Woman and her death-mate, and no other on board the skeleton ship. Like vessel, like crew!

"Her lips were red, her looks were free,
Her locks were yellow as gold:
Her skin was as white as leprosy,
The Nightmare Life-in-Death was she,
Who thicks men's blood with cold.

"The naked hulk alongside came,
And the twain were casting dice;
'The game is done! I've won! I've won!'
Quoth she, and whistles thrice.

Death and Life-in-Death have diced for the ship's crew, and she (the latter) winneth the ancient Mariner.

No twilight
within the
courts of the
Sun.

"The Sun's rim dips; the stars rush out;
At one stride comes the dark;
With far-heard whisper, o'er the sea,
Off shot the spectre-bark.

At the rising
of the Moon,

"We listened and looked sideways up!
Fear at my heart, as at a cup,
My life-blood seemed to sip!
The stars were dim, and thick the night,
The steersman's face by his lamp gleamed white,
From the sails the dew did drip—
Till clomb above the eastern bar
The hornèd Moon, with one bright star
Within the nether tip.

one after an-
other,

"One after one, by the star-dogged Moon,
Too quick for groan or sigh,
Each turned his face with a ghastly pang,
And cursed me with his eye.

his shipmates
drop down
dead.

"Four times fifty living men,
(And I heard nor sigh nor groan)
With heavy thump, a lifeless lump,
They dropped down one by one.

But Life-in-
Death begins
her work on
the ancient
Mariner.

"The souls did from their bodies fly,—
They fled to bliss or woe!
And every soul, it passed me by,
Like the whizz of my cross-bow!"

PART IV

"I fear thee, ancient Mariner!
I fear thy skinny hand!
And thou art long, and lank, and brown,
As is the ribbed sea-sand.

"I fear thee and thy glittering eye,
And thy skinny hand, so brown."—
"Fear not, fear not, thou Wedding-Guest!
This body dropt not down.

"Alone, alone, all, all alone,
Alone on a wide, wide sea!
And never a saint took pity on
My soul in agony.

"The many men, so beautiful!
And they all dead did lie:
And a thousand thousand slimy things
Lived on; and so did I.

"I looked upon the rotting sea,
And drew my eyes away;
I looked upon the rotting deck,
And there the dead men lay.

"I looked to heaven, and tried to pray;
But or ever a prayer had gusht,
A wicked whisper came, and made
My heart as dry as dust.

"I closed my lids, and kept them close,
And the balls like pulses beat;
For the sky and the sea, and the sea and the sky,
Lay like a load on my weary eye,
And the dead were at my feet.

The Wedding-Guest feareth that a spirit is talking to him; but the ancient

Mariner assureth him of his bodily life, and proceedeth to relate his horrible penance.

He despiseth the creatures of the calm,

and envieth that they should live, and so many be dead.

But the curse
liveth for him
in the eye of
the dead men.

"The cold sweat melted from their limbs,
Nor rot nor reek did they.
The look with which they looked on me
Had never passed away.

In his loneli-
ness and fixed-
ness he
yearneth to-
wards the
journeying
Moon, and
the stars that
still sojourn,
yet still move
onward; and
everywhere
the blue sky
belongs to
them, and is
their ap-
pointed rest,
and their
native coun-
try and their
own natural
homes, which
they enter
unannounced,
as lords that
are certainly
expected and
yet there is a
silent joy at
their arrival.

"An orphan's curse would drag to hell,
A spirit from on high;
But oh! more horrible than that
Is a curse in a dead man's eye!
Seven days, seven nights, I saw that curse,
And yet I could not die.

"The moving Moon went up the sky,
And nowhere did abide:
Softly she was going up,
And a star or two beside—

"Her beams bemocked the sultry main,
Like April hoar-frost spread;
But where the ship's huge shadow lay,
The charmèd water burnt alway
A still and awful red.

By the light
of the Moon
he beholdeth
God's crea-
tures of the
great calm

"Beyond the shadow of the ship,
I watched the water-snakes:
They moved in tracks of shining white,
And when they reared, the elfish light
Fell off in hoary flakes.

"Within the shadow of the ship
I watched their rich attire:
Blue, glossy green, and velvet black,
They coiled and swam; and every track
Was a flash of golden fire.

"O happy living things! no tongue
Their beauty might declare:
A spring of love gushed from my heart,
And I blessed them unaware:
Sure my kind saint took pity on me,
And I blessed them unaware.

Their beauty and their happiness.

He blesseth them in his heart.

"The selfsame moment I could pray;
And from my neck so free
The Albatross fell off, and sank
Like lead into the sea."

The spell begins to break.

PART V

"Oh sleep! it is a gentle thing,
Beloved from pole to pole!
To Mary Queen the praise be given!
She sent the gentle sleep from heaven,
That slid into my soul.

"The silly buckets on the deck,
That had so long remained,
I dreamt that they were filled with dew
And when I awoke, it rained.

By grace of the holy Mother, the ancient Mariner is refreshed with rain.

"My lips were wet, my throat was cold,
My garments all were dank;
Sure I had drunken in my dreams,
And still my body drank.

"I moved, and could not feel my limbs:
I was so light—almost
I thought that I had died in sleep,
And was a blessèd ghost.

He heareth
sounds and
seeth strange
sights and
commotions
in the sky and
the element.
"And soon I heard a roaring wind:
It did not come anear;
But with its sound it shook the sails,
That were so thin and sere.

"The upper air burst into life!
And a hundred fire-flags sheen,
To and fro they were hurried about!
And to and fro, and in and out,
The wan stars danced between.

"And the coming wind did roar more loud,
And the sails did sigh like sedge;
And the rain poured down from one black cloud;
The Moon was at its edge.

"The thick black cloud was cleft, and still
The Moon was at its side:
Like waters shot from some high crag,
The lightning fell with never a jag,
A river steep and wide.

The bodies of
the ship's
crew are in-
spirited, and
the ship
moves on;
"The loud wind never reached the ship,
Yet now the ship moved on!
Beneath the lightning and the Moon
The dead men gave a groan.

"They groaned, they stirred, they all uprose,
Nor spake, nor moved their eyes;
It had been strange, even in a dream,
To have seen those dead men rise.

"The helmsman steered, the ship moved on;
Yet never a breeze up blew;
The mariners all 'gan work the ropes,
Where they were wont to do;
They raised their limbs like lifeless tools—
We were a ghastly crew.

"The body of my brother's son
Stood by me, knee to knee:
The body and I pulled at one rope
But he said nought to me.—"

"I fear thee, ancient Mariner!"
"Be calm, thou Wedding-Guest!
'Twas not those souls that fled in pain,
Which to their corses came again,
But a troop of spirits blest:

but not by the
souls of the
men, nor by
dæmons of
earth or mid-
dle air, but by
a blessed
troop of
angelic spirits,
sent down by
the invocation
of the
guardian
saint.

"For when it dawned—they dropped their arms,
And clustered round the mast;
Sweet sounds rose slowly through their mouths
And from their bodies passed.

"Around, around, flew each sweet sound,
Then darted to the Sun;
Slowly the sounds came back again,
Now mixed, now one by one.

"Sometimes a-dropping from the sky
I heard the sky-lark sing;
Sometimes all the little birds that are,
How they seemed to fill the sea and air
With their sweet jargoning!

"And now 'twas like all instruments,
Now like a lonely flute;
And now it is an angel's song,
That makes the heavens be mute.

"It ceased; yet still the sails made on
A pleasant noise till noon,
A noise like of a hidden brook
In the leafy month of June,
That to the sleeping woods all night
Singeth a quiet tune.

"Till noon we quietly sailed on,
Yet never a breeze did breathe:
Slowly and smoothly went the ship,
Moved onward from beneath.

The lonesome Spirit from the south pole carries on the ship as far as the line, in obedience to the angelic troop, but still requireth vengeance.

"Under the keel nine fathom deep,
From the land of mist and snow,
The spirit slid; and it was he
That made the ship to go.
The sails at noon left off their tune,
And the ship stood still also.

"The Sun, right up above the mast,
Had fixed her to the ocean;
But in a minute she 'gan stir,
With a short uneasy motion—
Backwards and forwards half her length,
With a short uneasy motion.

"Then, like a pawing horse let go,
She made a sudden bound.
It flung the blood into my head,
And I fell down in a swound.

"How long in that same fit I lay,
I have not to declare;
But ere my living life returned,
I heard, and in my soul discerned,
Two voices in the air.

" 'Is it he?' quoth one, 'Is this the man?
By Him who died on cross,
With his cruel bow he laid full low
The harmless Albatross.

" 'The spirit who bideth by himself
In the land of mist and snow,
He loved the bird that loved the man
Who shot him with his bow.'

"The other was a softer voice,
As soft as honey-dew:
Quoth he, 'The man hath penance done,
And penance more will do.' "

The Polar
Spirit's fellow-
demons, the
invisible in-
habitants of
the element,
take part in
his wrong;
and two of
them relate,
one to the
other, that
penance long
and heavy
for the an-
cient Mariner
hath been ac-
corded to the
Polar Spirit,
who returneth
southward.

PART VI

First Voice

" 'But tell me, tell me! speak again,
Thy soft response renewing—
What makes that ship drive on so fast?
What is the ocean doing?'

Second Voice

" 'Still as a slave before his lord,
The ocean hath no blast;
His great bright eye most silently
Up to the Moon is cast—

" 'If he may know which way to go;
For she guides him smooth or grim.
See, brother, see! how graciously
She looketh down on him.'

First Voice

The Mariner
hath been cast
into a trance;
for the angelic
power causeth
the vessel to
drive north-
ward faster
than human
life could
endure.

" 'But why drives on that ship so fast,
Without or wave or wind?'

Second Voice

'The air is cut away before,
And closes from behind.

" 'Fly, brother, fly! more high, more high!
Or we shall be belated:
For slow and slow that ship will go,
When the Mariner's trance is abated.'

The super-
natural mo-
tion is re-
tarded; the
Mariner
awakes, and
his penance
begins anew.

"I woke, and we were sailing on
As in a gentle weather:
'Twas night, calm night, the Moon was high;
The dead men stood together.

"All stood together on the deck,
For a charnel-dungeon fitter:
All fixed on me their stony eyes,
That in the Moon did glitter.

"The pang, the curse, with which they died,
Had never passed away:
I could not draw my eyes from theirs,
Nor turn them up to pray.

"And now this spell was snapt: once more
I viewed the ocean green,
And looked far forth, yet little saw
Of what had else been seen—

The curse is
finally ex-
piated.

"Like one, that on a lonesome road
Doth walk in fear and dread,
And having once turned round walks on,
And turns no more his head;
Because he knows, a frightful fiend
Doth close behind him tread.

"But soon there breathed a wind on me
Nor sound nor motion made:
Its path was not upon the sea,
In ripple or in shade.

"It raised my hair, it fanned my cheek
Like a meadow-gale of spring—
It mingled strangely with my fears,
Yet it felt like a welcoming.

"Swiftly, swiftly flew the ship,
Yet she sailed softly too:
Sweetly, sweetly blew the breeze—
On me alone it blew.

"Oh! dream of joy! is this indeed
The lighthouse top I see?
Is this the hill? is this the kirk?
Is this mine own countree?

And the an-
cient Mariner
beholdeth his
native coun-
try.

"We drifted o'er the harbour-bar,
And I with sobs did pray—
'O let me be awake, my God!
Or let me sleep alway.'

"The harbour-bay was clear as glass,
So smoothly it was strewn!
And on the bay the moonlight lay,
And the shadow of the Moon.

"The rock shone bright, the kirk no less,
That stands above the rock:
The moonlight steeped in silentness
The steady weathercock.

"And the bay was white with silent light,
Till, rising from the same,
Full many shapes, that shadows were,
In crimson colours came.

The angelic
spirits leave
the dead
bodies,

and appear in
their own
forms of light.

"A little distance from the prow
Those crimson shadows were:
I turned my eyes upon the deck—
Oh Christ! what saw I there!

"Each corse lay flat, lifeless and flat,
And, by the holy rood!
A man all light, a seraph-man,
On every corse there stood.

"This seraph-band, each waved his hand:
It was a heavenly sight!
They stood as signals to the land,
Each one a lovely light;

"This seraph-band, each waved his hand.
No voice did they impart—
No voice; but oh! the silence sank
Like music on my heart.

"But soon I heard the dash of oars;
I heard the Pilot's cheer;
My head was turned perforce away,
And I saw a boat appear.

"The Pilot and the Pilot's boy,
I heard them coming fast:
Dear Lord in Heaven! it was a joy
The dead men could not blast.

"I saw a third—I heard his voice:
It is the Hermit good!
He singeth loud his godly hymns
That he makes in the wood.
He'll shrieve my soul, he'll wash away
The Albatross's blood."

PART VII

"This Hermit good lives in that wood
Which slopes down to the sea.
How loudly his sweet voice he rears!
He loves to talk with marineres
That come from a far countree.

"He kneels at morn, and noon, and eve—
He hath a cushion plump:
It is the moss that wholly hides
The rotted old oak-stump.

The Hermit
of the wood

"The skiff-boat neared: I heard them talk
'Why, this is strange, I trow!
Where are those lights so many and fair,
That signal made but now?'

approacheth
the ship with
wonder.

" 'Strange, by my faith!' the Hermit said—
'And they answered not our cheer!
The planks look warped! and see those sails,
How thin they are and sere!
I never saw aught like to them,
Unless perchance it were

" 'Brown skeletons of leaves that lag
My forest-brook along;
When the ivy-tod is heavy with snow,
And the owlet whoops to the wolf below,
That eats the she-wolf's young.'

" 'Dear Lord! it hath a fiendish look—'
(The Pilot made reply)
'I am a-feared'—'Push on, push on!'
Said the Hermit cheerily.

"The boat came closer to the ship,
But I nor spake nor stirred;
The boat came close beneath the ship,
And straight a sound was heard.

The ship sud-
denly sinketh.

"Under the water it rumbled on,
Still louder and more dread:
It reached the ship, it split the bay;
The ship went down like lead.

"Stunned by that loud and dreadful sound,
Which sky and ocean smote,
Like one that hath been seven days drowned
My body lay afloat;
But, swift as dreams, myself I found
Within the Pilot's boat.

The ancient
Mariner is
saved in the
Pilot's boat.

"Upon the whirl, where sank the ship,
The boat spun round and round;
And all was still, save that the hill
Was telling of the sound.

"I moved my lips—the Pilot shrieked
And fell down in a fit;
The holy Hermit raised his eyes,
And prayed where he did sit.

"I took the oars: the Pilot's boy,
Who now doth crazy go,
Laughed loud and long, and all the while
His eyes went to and fro.
'Ha! ha!' quoth he, 'full plain I see,
The Devil knows how to row.'

"And now, all in my own countree,
I stood on the firm land!
The Hermit stepped forth from the boat.
And scarcely he could stand.

" 'O shrieve me, shrieve me, holy man!'
The Hermit crossed his brow
'Say quick,' quoth he, 'I bid thee say—
What manner of man art thou?'

The ancient
Mariner ear-
nestly en-
treateth the
Hermit to
shrieve him;
and the pen-
ance of life
falls on him.

"Forthwith this frame of mine was wrenched
With a woful agony,
Which forced me to begin my tale;
And then it left me free.

And ever and
anon through-
out his future
life an agony
constraineth
him to travel
from land to
land,
"Since then, at an uncertain hour,
That agony returns;
And till my ghastly tale is told,
This heart within me burns.

"I pass, like night, from land to land;
I have strange power of speech;
That moment that his face I see,
I know the man that must hear me:
To him my tale I teach.

"What loud uproar bursts from that door!
The wedding-guests are there:
But in the garden-bower the bride
And bride-maids singing are:
And hark the little vesper bell,
Which biddeth me to prayer!

"O Wedding-Guest! this soul hath been
Alone on a wide, wide sea:
So lonely 'twas, that God himself
Scarce seemèd there to be.

"O sweeter than the marriage-feast,
'Tis sweeter far to me,
To walk together to the kirk
With a goodly company!—

"To walk together to the kirk,
And all together pray,
While each to his great Father bends,
Old men, and babes, and loving friends,
And youths and maidens gay!

"Farewell, farewell! but this I tell
To thee, thou Wedding-Guest!
He prayeth well, who loveth well
Both man and bird and beast.

and to teach,
by his own
example, love
and reverence
to all things
that God
made and
loveth.

"He prayeth best, who loveth best
All things both great and small;
For the dear God who loveth us,
He made and loveth all."

The Mariner, whose eye is bright,
Whose beard with age is hoar,
Is gone: and now the Wedding-Guest
Turned from the bridegroom's door.

He went like one that hath been stunned,
And is of sense forlorn:
A sadder and a wiser man
He rose the morrow morn.

Levels of Meaning and Figures of Speech

As we read this poem for the first time, we tell ourselves that it is
the account of a voyage on a ship that crosses the equator and
finally returns to its home port after a number of strange oc-
currences—in accordance with the "Argument" (in this instance
meaning "subject matter"). This is its obvious theme. Even as a

sea-story the poem is exciting, if not unusually mysterious. The supernatural incidents and the behavior of the Mariner suggest, however, to the reader that more is involved than the vivid tabulation of events. To grasp the full significance of what is being said, one must probe for another level of meaning. The poem concerns a journey, yes—but not simply a journey in the physical world. It is the journey, rather, of a tormented soul forced to travel "like night, from land to land," through a purgatory of horrors before coming to rest.

In its deeper meaning, this poem strongly suggests a moral; it concerns the choice between good and evil, a choice that is the subject of much great literature. The Mariner chooses the course of evil, and this leaves him no room for the love of God's creatures. From the time he commits the deed which epitomizes his abandonment of humanitarian principles—the wanton killing of the albatross—until he begins to regain the feeling of love, he drifts tormented in a fantastic world of terror. Even after the curse is broken, the Ancient Mariner must continue to atone for his former sins. The penance? Telling his story to anyone he believes will benefit from his experience. It is with just such a recital that the narrative begins.

In this poem Coleridge employs the ballad stanza, using an occasional variation in length. But the concept is grander than that of the popular ballad. Color, sound, and movement are made to come tumbling at us through the poet's "figurative language" and especial skill with evocative devices of sound.

Not all figures of speech make comparisons, but those in *The Ancient Mariner* we are concerned with do—metaphor, simile, and personification. These make the unknown comprehensible; they explain. How many times, for instance, do we hear people start a story by saying, "It's like this . . . ," or words to that effect? This is just what the poet does when he uses figures of comparison. If he employs a simile, he will introduce it with "like," "as," or another word indicating comparison. For example:

> The bride hath paced into the hall
> Red as a rose is she.

Metaphor differs from simile. You can tell them apart simply by remembering that metaphor is not introduced by "like," "as," or similar words. Whereas similes pinpoint resemblances, with metaphors the effect is achieved through contrast, an interrelation of opposites. And for this reason metaphors are usually more complicated than similes. We can say that a simile is explicit, while a metaphor is implicit. The metaphor in these lines,

> And every tongue, through utter drought
> Was withered at the root,

compares men who are parched with plants drying up for lack of rain. It is, as metaphors go, a fairly obvious one. Sometimes, if the metaphor or simile is elaborate and makes a point-by-point comparison, it is termed "allegory."

Personification is a particular kind of metaphor. It occurs when the characteristics of a human being are applied to an animal, an object, or to an idea.

> The sun came up upon the left,
> Out of the sea came he!
> And he shone bright, and on the right
> Went down into the sea.

And again:

> The moving moon went up the sky
> And nowhere did abide!
> Softly she was going up,
> And a star or two beside—

In the first of these two stanzas we see the sun assigned its traditionally masculine role, whereas in the second the customary feminine characteristics are ascribed to the moon.

Sometimes the poet names a person or thing by some other word that suggests or resembles it (metonymy). In the line

(Heaven's Mother send us grace!)

the word "Heaven," His dwelling place, is substituted for Christ. In so doing the poet causes an entire concept to grow in significance. In this particular instance the popularity of the cult of the Virgin Mary is emphasized and gives to the poem a flavor appropriate to an earlier period of history, since it was in the Middle Ages that the veneration of the Virgin was at its height. It is to establish this same illusion of antiquity that Coleridge uses archaic language. He also provides marginal comments—a practice employed, before Coleridge's day, to explain textual difficulties in ancient works that had come to light. Remember that the poem itself was first published in 1798.

Occasionally the poet makes a part of something stand for the whole (synecdoche), as in

The western wave was all aflame. . . .

Here "wave," a part of the ocean, symbolizes as much of the ocean as can be seen. This line contains a metaphor in the word "aflame," as well as another device Coleridge uses expertly— alliteration—that is, the repetition of identical consonant sounds. The following alliterative lines are among the most famous in English literature:

The fair breeze blew, the white foam flew,
The furrow followed free. . . .

Onomatopoeia occurs when the sound of a word suggests its meaning; it is often used in *The Rime of the Ancient Mariner*. For example:

It *cracked* and *growled*, and *roared* and *howled*

and:

Like the *whizz* of my cross-bow!

Metrical variations, as you have seen, prevent monotony, but it is not enough to substitute a foot, or metrical unit, for this reason alone. The substituted foot—one different from that of the regular meter of the poem—must create a special effect, whether to emphasize or to imitate a particular movement. The anapests (two unstressed syllables followed by one stressed syllable) of this stanza suggest the monotony of the endless sea and the endless sky:

> Ĭ clośed my lĭds, ănd képt thĕm clóse,
> Ănd thĕ bálls lĭke púlsĕs bĕat;
> Fŏr thĕ sky ănd thĕ séa, ănd thĕ séa ănd thĕ sky,
> Láy lĭke ă lóad ŏn my wéarў éye,
> Ănd thĕ déad wĕre ăt my féet.

In the following stanza we find the irregularity of the lines gives emphasis:

> Ălóne, ălóne, áll, áll ălóne,
> Ălóne ŏn ă wíde, wíde séa!
> Ănd néver ă saint took pítў oń
> My sóul ĭn ágonў.

Only a few of the figures of speech and other subtleties that abound in this poem have been touched on, but they should be enough to lead you to search out others. Then the reading of this poem, like the reading of any good poem, will become an experience of discovery.

A more recent literary ballad is "Danny Deever," by Rudyard Kipling (1865–1936):

Danny Deever[1]

"What are the bugles blowin' for?" said Files-on-Parade.
"To turn you out, to turn you out," the Colour-Sergeant said.
"What makes you look so white, so white?" said Files-on-Parade.
"I'm dreadin' what I've got to watch," the Colour-Sergeant said.
　　For they're hangin' Danny Deever, you can hear the Dead
　　　　March play,
　　The Regiment's in 'ollow square—they're hangin' him to-day;
　　They've taken of his buttons off an' cut his stripes away,
　　An' they're hangin' Danny Deever in the mornin'.

"What makes the rear-rank breathe so 'ard?" said Files-on-Parade.
"It's bitter cold, it's bitter cold," the Colour-Sergeant said.
"What makes that front-rank man fall down?" said Files-on-
　　Parade.
"A touch o' sun, a touch o' sun," the Colour-Sergeant said.
　　They are hangin' Danny Deever, they are marchin' of 'im
　　　　round,
　　They 'ave 'alted Danny Deever by 'is coffin on the ground;
　　An' 'e'll swing in 'arf a minute for a sneakin' shootin' hound—
　　O they're hangin' Danny Deever in the mornin'!

" 'Is cot was right-'and cot to mine," said Files-on-Parade.
" 'E's sleepin' out an' far to-night," the Colour-Sergeant said.
"I've drunk 'is beer a score o' times," said Files-on-Parade.
" 'E's drinkin' bitter beer alone," the Colour-Sergeant said.
　　They are hangin' Danny Deever, you must mark 'im to 'is
　　　　place,
　　For 'e shot a comrade sleepin'—you must look 'im in the face;
　　Nine 'undred of 'is county an' the Regiment's disgrace,
　　While they're hangin' Danny Deever in the mornin'.

　　[1] From *Departmental Ditties* by Rudyard Kipling. Reprinted by permission of Mrs. George Bambridge and Doubleday & Company, Inc.

"What's that so black agin the sun?" said Files-on-Parade.
"It's Danny fightin' 'ard for life," the Colour-Sergeant said.
"What's that that whimpers over'ead?" said Files-on-Parade.
"It's Danny's soul that's passin' now," the Colour-Sergeant said.
For they're done with Danny Deever, you can 'ear the quick-
    step play,
The Regiment's in column, an' they're marchin' us away;
Ho! the young recruits are shakin', an' they'll want their
    beer today,
After hangin' Danny Deever in the mornin'!

This poem is written in eight-line stanzas. Each line is sep-
tenary—that is, a seven-foot line of four stressed syllables, a
grammatical pause called a "caesura," and then three more stressed
syllables.

Through the rhythm he uses, Kipling manages to give the
impression of a soldierly marching tempo; by the choppy quality
of his choice of words, too, he sets a pace suggestive of the movement of troops in formation. This pace quickens as the climax
of the narrative nears:

" 'Is cot was right-'and cot to mine," said Files-on-Parade.

"Danny Deever" is in the oral tradition of the ballad, in that
what is being said can be taken in at one hearing. This singleness
of impression is achieved by the poet's skill in combining words
so that none stands out to detract from the total impression.
Words, sounds, and rhythm—all lead evenly to the climax. We
term this "unity of impression"—a fundamental goal in art.

To be assured that the popular ballad tradition is not dead
all one needs do is examine the Calypso songs of the Caribbean.
One of the best known among them is called "Well, It's Love,
Love Alone," which takes a significant political event with ro-
mantic overtones and makes it the subject of a narrative. With
its repetition, generally steady iambics, and reliance on language

that is not figurative, it is only in a topical way that this piece
differs from the ballads of centuries ago; the event it records
occurred as recently as 1936. The author's name is no longer
known.

Well, It's Love, Love Alone[2]

Well, it's love, love alone
Caused King Edward to leave his throne.
It was love, love, love, love alone
Caused King Edward to leave his throne.

On de tenth of December we heard de talk:
He gave his throne to de Duke of York.
It was love, love, love, love alone
Caused King Edward to leave his throne.

King Edward was noble; King Edward was great.
It was love caused him to abdicate.
It was love, love, love, love alone
Caused King Edward to leave his throne.

He said he was sorry dat his mommy would grieve.
He could not help it; he would have to leave.
It was love, love, love, love alone
Caused King Edward to leave his throne.

You can take his cow; you can take his goat,
Leave him with his yachting boat.
It was love, love, love, love alone
Caused King Edward to leave his throne.

You can take his money; you can take his store,
Or give him that lady from Baltimore.
It was love, love, love, love alone
Caused King Edward to leave his throne.

I don't know what dis Simpson got in her bone
Dat caused de King to leave his throne.
It was love, love, love, love alone
Caused King Edward to leave his throne.

On de tenth of December nineteen-thirty-six
De Duke of Windsor went to get his kicks.
It was love, love, love, love alone
Caused King Edward to leave his throne.

2

The Art of Tragedy

Although many theories and definitions of tragedy exist, a few fundamental principles are generally accepted. In the first place, to elicit our sympathy the hero, or protagonist, as he is often called, must be admired because of his courage, honor, or some other virtue; or we must sympathize with his plight, as in *Macbeth*. In a tragedy the protagonist usually meets an unhappy fate. There may be some weakness in his nature that he is unable to overcome, or if he is youthful and inexperienced, he may die because of the misunderstanding or indifference of those about him. Perhaps, as in classical Greek tragedy, what happens to him is ordained by Fate. But whatever the cause, in the great tragedies the conflict of good and evil within the protagonist is frequently greater than any external obstacle he has to face.

Near the beginning of a tragedy there is frequently a sense of foreboding; the reader is thus warned that the outcome will be unhappy. Were we to have no prior suspicion about the fate of the protagonist, suspense would be lacking, and we would be so unprepared for what follows that the climax would lose its force.

Climax is the high point, the most intense moment, of action; the suspense of the drama ceases at the climax. What follows is the denouement, or the clarification, of all the events preceding the climax.

"Out, Out," a short, dramatic narrative by Robert Frost (1875–1963), contains the main traditional elements of tragic writing.

Out, Out[1]

The buzz-saw snarled and rattled in the yard
And made dust and dropped stove-length sticks of wood,
Sweet-scented stuff when the breeze drew across it.
And from there those that lifted eyes could count
Five mountain ranges one behind the other
Under the sunset far into Vermont.
And the saw snarled and rattled, snarled and rattled,
As it ran light, or had to bear a load.
And nothing happened: day was all but done.
Call it a day, I wish they might have said
To please the boy by giving him the half hour
That a boy counts so much when saved from work.
His sister stood beside them in her apron
To tell them "Supper." At the word, the saw,
As if to prove saws knew what supper meant,
Leaped out at the boy's hand, or seemed to leap—
He must have given the hand. However it was,
Neither refused the meeting. But the hand!
The boy's first outcry was a rueful laugh,
As he swung toward them holding up the hand
Half in appeal, but half as if to keep
The life from spilling. Then the boy saw all—

[1] From *Complete Poems of Robert Frost*. Copyright 1916, 1921 by Holt, Rinehart and Winston, Inc.; copyright 1944 by Robert Frost; reprinted by permission of Holt, Rinehart and Winston, Inc.

Since he was old enough to know, big boy
Doing a man's work, though a child at heart—
He saw all spoiled. "Don't let him cut my hand off—
The doctor, when he comes. Don't let him, sister!"
So. But the hand was gone already.
The doctor put him in the dark of ether.
He lay and puffed his lips out with his breath.
And then—the watcher at his pulse took fright.
No one believed. They listened at his heart.
Little—less—nothing!—and that ended it.
No more to build on there. And they, since they
Were not the one dead, turned to their affairs.

In the first line of this poem the saw is personified by the word "snarled"; at once it becomes the antagonist or villain in the drama. The repetition of this threatening word in the onomatopoetic seventh line prepares us like a danger signal for the tragedy about to occur.

When the poet says:

Call it a day, I wish they might have said
To please the boy by giving him the half hour
That a boy counts so much when saved from work. . . .

we see that the tragedy need not have happened. The accident was the indirect result of adult thoughtlessness, however innocent. The climax comes swiftly, and the deliberate flatness of the denouement saves a melodramatic situation from mawkishness. The theme of the story, that one's duty is to endure, is stated here.

The source of the title, Macbeth's soliloquy in Act V, enhances the irony in the poem. Macbeth cries: "Out, out, brief candle," at the end of a life that has been diverted from its original course; in Frost's poem, it is the boy's life that is snuffed out almost before it has begun.

Much of the power of the poem lies in its bareness of outline, sharp as the

Five mountain ranges one behind the other.

This impression is enhanced by Frost's blank verse; the many pauses and elliptical expressions are typical of his narrator, who is not verbally up to the emotion the situation demands. This, the laconic style of country folk, gives Frost's work its peculiarly individual inflection—a seasoning of rusticity, of conversational yet precise psychology, of quiet, sometimes dramatic observation and protest. The casual, almost shuffling manner of some of his poems sometimes belies their technical astringency. It is by relating those values that were his deepest concern to living people, to everyday situations, that Frost has been able to give his personal revelations their persuasiveness and authenticity.

The Epic

Like the ballad, the epic is of two kinds, but described as oral and written rather than popular and literary. The oral epic evolves early in a people's history—for example, the *Odyssey* of the Greeks, the *Chanson de Roland* of the French, and the English *Beowulf* and Arthurian legends. The written epic follows the style and purpose of the oral, but its authorship is usually known. Among the most famous are Vergil's *Aeneid*, Dante's *Divine Comedy*, Camoëns' *Lusiads*, and Milton's *Paradise Lost*. Epics are still written today; many of you will read *John Brown's Body*, for example, Stephen Vincent Benét's epic about the American Civil War.

The epic is usually a long, dignified, rhythmic narrative, with a momentous theme involving heroic characters and supernatural agencies under the control of a sovereign destiny. In this definition, which demands rather careful analysis, "dignified" refers to style and content; by using this term we mean that the epic is worthy of man's contemplation, because what is said and how it is said are lofty and significant. Most English epics are written in blank verse—unrhyming metrical lines that are usually iambic pentameter. If the poet were to rhyme his epic, he would impose on himself considerable restrictions, and the many rhymes necessary would soon become tiresome and unnatural to the reader. The epic is of course rhythmic; otherwise it could as well be written in the form of a historical novel.

A narrative tells a story. In most epics the story concerns the deeds of a national hero and what he undergoes for the good of his people. The supernatural plays a large role in early epics. Above all, it is Fate or One God who cannot be shaken from his resolve that reigns. What eventually occurs has been destined to happen from the very beginning, and no force, however strong, can alter it.

Sohrab and Rustum by the English poet Matthew Arnold (1822–1888), based on a Persian epic about the hero Rustum, is the account of a single incident from the much longer (Persian) work. In Arnold's poem not only the character and style of the epic are to be found, but all the elements of tragedy as well. The poet terms what he describes an episode, and indeed the episodic nature of the poem is pointed out by the way it starts out with the word "and." We are thus introduced to something already under way.

Sohrab and Rustum

AN EPISODE

And the first grey of morning filled the east,
And the fog rose out of the Oxus stream.
But all the Tartar camp along the stream
Was hushed, and still the men were plunged in sleep.
Sohrab alone, he slept not; all night long   5

He had lain wakeful, tossing on his bed:
But when the grey dawn stole into his tent,
He rose, and clad himself, and girt his sword,
And took his horseman's cloak, and left his tent,
And went abroad into the cold wet fog,   10
Through the dim camp to Peran-Wisa's tent.
    Through the black Tartar tents he passed, which stood
Clustering like bee-hives on the low flat strand
Of Oxus, where the summer-floods o'erflow
When the sun melts the snows in high Pamere;   15
Through the black tents he passed, o'er that low strand.
And to a hillock came, a little back
From the stream's brink,—the spot where first a boat,
Crossing the stream in summer, scrapes the land.
The men of former times had crowned the top   20
With a clay fort; but that was fallen, and now
The Tartars built there Peran-Wisa's tent,
A dome of laths, and o'er it felts were spread.
And Sohrab came there, and went in, and stood
Upon the thick piled carpets in the tent,   25
And found the old man sleeping on his bed
Of rugs and felts, and near him lay his arms.
And Peran-Wisa heard him, though the step
Was dulled; for he slept light, an old man's sleep;
And he rose quickly on one arm, and said,—   30
    "Who art thou? for it is not yet clear dawn.
Speak! is there news, or any night alarm?"
    But Sohrab came to the bedside, and said,—
"Thou know'st me, Peran-Wisa! it is I.
The sun has not yet risen, and the foe   35
Sleep: but I sleep not; all night long I lie
Tossing and wakeful, and I come to thee.
For so did King Afrasiab bid me seek
Thy counsel, and to heed thee as thy son,

In Samarcand, before the army marched;   40
And I will tell thee what my heart desires.
Thou know'st if, since from Ader-baijan first
I came among the Tartars, and bore arms,
I have still served Afrasiab well, and shown,
At my boy's years, the courage of a man.   45
This too thou know'st, that while I still bear on
The conquering Tartar ensigns through the world,
And beat the Persians back on every field,
I seek one man, one man, and one alone,—
Rustum, my father; who I hoped should greet,   50
Should one day greet, upon some well-fought field,
His not unworthy, not inglorious son.
So I long hoped, but him I never find.
Come then, hear now, and grant me what I ask.
Let the two armies rest to-day; but I   55
Will challenge forth the bravest Persian lords
To meet me, man to man: if I prevail,
Rustum will surely hear it; if I fall—
Old man, the dead need no one, claim no kin.
Dim is the rumour of a common fight   60
Where host meets host, and many names are sunk;
But of a single combat fame speaks clear."
     He spoke; and Persan-Wisa took the hand
Of the young man in his, and sighed, and said,—
     "O Sohrab, an unquiet heart is thine!   65
Canst thou not rest among the Tartar chiefs,
And share the battle's common chance with us
Who love thee, but must press forever first,
In single fight incurring single risk,
To find a father thou hast never seen?   70
That were far best, my son, to stay with us
Unmurmuring; in our tents, while it is war,
And when 'tis truce, then in Afrasiab's towns.

But if this one desire indeed rules all,
To seek out Rustum—seek him not through fight!   75
Seek him in peace, and carry to his arms,
O Sohrab, carry an unwounded son!
But far hence seek him, for he is not here.
For now it is not as when I was young,
When Rustum was in front of every fray: 80
But now he keeps apart, and sits at home,
In Seistan, with Zal, his father old;
Whether that his own mighty strength at last
Feels the abhorred approaches of old age;
Or in some quarrel with the Persian king.   85
There go!—Thou wilt not? Yet my heart forebodes
Danger or death awaits thee on this field.
Fain would I know thee safe and well, though lost
To us; fain therefore send thee hence in peace
To seek thy father, not seek single fights   90
In vain. But who can keep the lion's cub
From ravening, and who govern Rustum's son?
Go: I will grant thee what thy heart desires."
      So said he, and dropped Sohrab's hand, and left
His bed, and the warm rugs whereon he lay;   95
And o'er his chilly limbs his woollen coat
He passed, and tied his sandals on his feet,
And threw a white cloak round him, and he took
In his right hand a ruler's staff, no sword;
And on his head he set his sheep-skin cap,   100
Black, glossy, curled, the fleece of Kara-Kul;
And raised the curtain of his tent, and called
His herald to his side, and went abroad.
      The sun by this had risen, and cleared the fog
From the broad Oxus and the glittering sands.   105
And from their tents the Tartar horsemen filed
Into the open plain: so Haman bade,—

Haman, who next to Peran-Wisa ruled
The host, and still was in his lusty prime.
From their black tents, long files of horse, they streamed;   110
As when some grey November morn the files,
In marching order spread, of long-necked cranes
Stream over Casbin and the southern slopes
Of Elburz, from the Aralian estuaries,
Or some frore Caspian reed-bed, southward bound   115
For the warm Persian seaboard,—so they streamed.
The Tartars of the Oxus, the king's guard,
First, with black sheep-skin caps and with long spears;
Large men, large steeds, who from Bokhara came
And Khiva, and ferment the milk of mares.   120
Next, the more temperate Toorkmuns of the south,
The Tukas, and the lances of Salore,
And those from Attruck and the Caspian sands;
Light men on light steeds, who only drink
The acrid milk of camels, and their wells.   125
And then a swarm of wandering horse, who came
From far, and a more doubtful service owned,—
The Tartars of Ferghana, from the banks
Of the Jaxartes, men with scanty beards
And close-set skull-caps; and those wilder hordes   130
Who roam o'er Kipchak and the northern waste,
Kalmucks and unkempt Kuzzaks, tribes who stray
Nearest the pole, and wandering Kirghizzes,
Who come on shaggy ponies from Pamere,—
These all filed out from camp into the plain.   135
And on the other side the Persians formed,—
First a light cloud of horse, Tartars they seemed,
The Ilyats of Khorassan; and behind,
The royal troops of Persia, horse and foot,
Marshalled battalions bright in burnished steel.   140
But Peran-Wisa with his herald came,

Threading the Tartar squadrons to the front,
And with his staff kept back the foremost ranks.
And when Ferood, who led the Persians, saw
That Peran-Wisa kept the Tartars back,   145
He took his spear, and to the front he came,
And checked his ranks, and fixed them where they stood.
And the old Tartar came upon the sand
Betwixt the silent hosts, and spake, and said,—
    "Ferood, and ye, Persians and Tartars, hear!   150
Let there be truce between the hosts to-day.
But choose a champion from the Persian lords
To fight our champion Sohrab, man to man."
    As in the country, on a morn in June,
When the dew glistens on the pearled ears,   155
A shiver runs through the deep corn for joy,—
So, when they heard what Peran-Wisa said,
A thrill through all the Tartar squadrons ran
Of pride and hope for Sohrab, whom they loved.
    But as a troop of pedlars from Cabool   160
Cross underneath the Indian Caucasus,
That vast sky-neighbouring mountain of milk snow:
Crossing so high, that, as they mount, they pass
Long flocks of travelling birds dead on the snow,
Choked by the air, and scarce can they themselves   165
Slake their parched throats with sugared mulberries;
In single file they move, and stop their breath,
For fear they should dislodge the o'erhanging snows,—
So the pale Persians held their breath with fear.
    And to Ferood his brother chiefs came up   170
To counsel; Gudurz and Zoarrah came,
And Feraburz, who ruled the Persian host
Second, and was the uncle of the king;
These came and counselled, and then Gudurz said,—
    "Ferood, shame bids us take their challenge up,   175

Yet champion have we none to match this youth.
He has the wild stag's foot, the lion's heart.
But Rustum came last night; aloof he sits
And sullen, and has pitched his tents apart.
Him will I seek, and carry to his ear   180
The Tartar challenge, and this young man's name;
Haply he will forget his wrath, and fight.
Stand forth the while, and take their challenge up."
    So spake he; and Ferood stood forth and cried,—
"Old man, be it agreed as thou hast said!   185
Let Sohrab arm, and we will find a man."
    He spake; and Peran-Wisa turned, and strode
Back through the opening squadrons to his tent.
But through the anxious Persians Gudurz ran,
And crossed the camp which lay behind, and reached,   190
Out on the sands beyond it, Rustum's tents.
Of scarlet cloth they were, and glittering gay,
Just pitched; the high pavilion in the midst
Was Rustum's, and his men lay camped around.
And Gudurz entered Rustum's tent, and found   195
Rustum; his morning meal was done, but still
The table stood before him, charged with food,—
A side of roasted sheep, and cakes of bread,
And dark-green melons; and there Rustum sate
Listless, and held a falcon on his wrist,   200
And played with it; but Gudurz came and stood
Before him; and he looked, and saw him stand,
And with a cry sprang up, and dropped the bird,
And greeted Gudurz with both hands, and said,—
    "Welcome! these eyes could see no better sight.   205
What news? but sit down first, and eat and drink."
    But Gudurz stood in the tent-door, and said,—
"Not now. A time will come to eat and drink,
But not to-day: to-day has other needs.

The armies are drawn out, and stand at gaze;   210
For, from the Tartars is a challenge brought
To pick a champion from the Persian lords
To fight their champion—and thou know'st his name:
Sohrab men call him, but his birth is hid.
O Rustum, like thy might is this young man's!   215
He has the wild stag's foot, the lion's heart;
And he is young, and Iran's chiefs are old,
Or else too weak; and all eyes turn to thee.
Come down and help us, Rustum, or we lose!"
    He spoke; but Rustum answered with a smile,—   220
"Go to! if Iran's chiefs are old, then I
Am older. If the young are weak, the king
Errs strangely; for the king, for Kai Khosroo,
Himself is young, and honours younger men,
And lets the aged moulder to their graves.   225
Rustum he loves no more, but loves the young:
The young may rise at Sohrab's vaunts, not I.
For what care I, though all speak Sohrab's fame?
For would that I myself had such a son,
And not that one slight helpless girl I have!   230
A son so famed, so brave, to send to war,
And I to tarry with the snow-haired Zal,
My father, whom the robber Afghans vex,
And clip his borders short, and drive his herds,
And he has none to guard his weak old age.   235
There would I go, and hang my armour up,
And with my great name fence that weak old man,
And spend the goodly treasures I have got,
And rest my age, and hear of Sohrab's fame,
And leave to death the hosts of thankless kings,   240
And with these slaughterous hands draw sword no more."
    He spoke, and smiled; and Gudurz made reply,
"What then, O Rustum, will men say to this,

When Sohrab dares our bravest forth, and seeks
Thee most of all, and thou, whom he most seeks,   245
Hidest thy face? Take heed lest men should say,—
Like some old miser, Rustum hoards his fame,
And shuns to peril it with younger men."
And, greatly moved, then Rustum made reply,—
"O Gudurz, wherefore dost thou say such words?   250
Thou knowest better words than this to say.
What is one more, one less, obscure or famed,
Valiant or craven, young or old, to me?
Are not they mortal? am not I myself?
But who for men of naught would do great deeds?   255
Come, thou shalt see how Rustum hoards his fame!
But I will fight unknown, and in plain arms:
Let not men say of Rustum, he was matched
In single fight with any mortal man."
    He spoke, and frowned; and Gudurz turned, and ran   260
Back quickly through the camp in fear and joy,—
Fear at his wrath, but joy that Rustum came.
But Rustum strode to his tent-door, and called
His followers in, and bade them bring his arms,
And clad himself in steel. The arms he chose   265
Were plain, and on his shield was no device;
Only his helm was rich, inlaid with gold,
And, from the fluted spine a-top, a plume
Of horse-hair waved, a scarlet horse-hair plume.
So armed, he issued forth; and Ruksh, his horse,   270
Followed him like a faithful hound at heel,—
Ruksh, whose renown was noised through all the earth,
The horse whom Rustum on a foray once
Did in Bokhara by the river find
A colt beneath its dam, and drove him home,   275
And reared him; a bright bay, with lofty crest,
Dight with a saddle-cloth of broidered green

Crusted with gold, and on the ground were worked
All beasts of chase, all beasts which hunters know.
So followed, Rustum left his tents, and crossed   280
The camp, and to the Persian host appeared.
And all the Persians knew him, and with shouts
Hailed; but the Tartars knew not who he was.
And dear as the wet diver to the eyes
Of his pale wife who waits and weeps on shore,   285
By sandy Bahrein, in the Persian Gulf,
Plunging all day in the blue waves, at night,
Having made up his tale of precious pearls
Rejoins her in their hut upon the sands,—
So dear to the pale Persians Rustum came.   290
    And Rustum to the Persian front advanced;
And Sohrab armed in Hamans' tent, and came.
And as a-field the reapers cut a swath
Down through the middle of a rich man's corn,
And on each side are squares of standing corn,   295
And in the midst a stubble short and bare,—
So on each side were squares of men, with spears
Bristling, and in the midst the open sand.
And Rustum came upon the sand, and cast
His eyes toward the Tartar tents, and saw   300
Sohrab come forth, and eyed him as he came.
    As some rich woman, on a winter's morn,
Eyes through her silken curtains the poor drudge
Who with numb blackened fingers makes her fire,—
At cock-crow, on a starlit winter's morn,   305
When the frost flowers the whitened window-panes,—
And wonders how she lives, and what the thoughts
Of that poor drudge may be; so Rustum eyed
The unknown adventurous youth, who from afar
Came seeking Rustum, and defying forth   310
All the most valiant chiefs; long he perused

His spirited air, and wondered who he was.
For very young he seemed, tenderly reared;
Like some young cypress, tall and dark and straight,
Which in a queen's secluded garden throws   315
Its slight dark shadow on a moonlit turf,
By midnight, to a bubbling fountain's sound,—
So slender Sohrab seemed, so softly reared.
And a deep pity entered Rustum's soul
As he beheld him coming; and he stood,   320
And beckoned to him with his hand; and said,—
     "O thou young man, the air of heaven is soft,
And warm, and pleasant; but the grave is cold!
Heaven's air is better than the cold dead grave.
Behold me! I am vast, and clad in iron,   325
And tried; and I have stood on many a field
Of blood, and I have fought with many a foe:
Never was that field lost, or that foe saved.
O Sohrab, wherefore wilt thou rush on death?
Be governed: quit the Tartar host, and come   330
To Iran, and be as my son to me,
And fight beneath my banner till I die!
There are no youths in Iran brave as thou."
     So he spake, mildly. Sohrab heard his voice,
The mighty voice of Rustum, and he saw   335
His giant figure planted on the sand,
Sole, like some single tower, which a chief
Hath builded on the waste in former years
Against the robbers; and he saw that head,
Streaked with its first grey hairs; hope filled his soul,   340
And he ran forward, and embraced his knees,
And clasped his hand within his own, and said,—
     "Oh, by thy father's head! by thine own soul!
Art thou not Rustum? Speak! art thou not he?"
     But Rustum eyed askance the kneeling youth,   345

And turned away, and spake to his own soul,—
  "Ah me! I muse what this young fox may mean!
False, wily, boastful, are these Tartar boys.
For if I now confess this thing he asks,
And hide it not, but say, *Rustum is here!*   350
He will not yield indeed, nor quit our foes;
But he will find some pretext not to fight,
And praise my fame, and proffer courteous gifts,
A belt or sword perhaps, and go his way.
And on a feast-tide, in Afrasiab's hall   355
In Samarcand, he will arise and cry,—
  'I challenged once, when the two armies camped
Beside the Oxus, all the Persian lords
To cope with me in single fight; but they
Shrank, only Rustum dared; then he and I   360
Changed gifts, and went on equal terms away.'
So will he speak, perhaps, while men applaud;
Then were the chiefs of Iran shamed through me."
  And then he turned, and sternly spake aloud,—
"Rise! wherefore dost thou vainly question thus   365
Of Rustum? I am here, whom thou hast called
By challenge forth; make good thy vaunt, or yield!
Is it with Rustum only thou wouldst fight?
Rash boy, men look on Rustum's face, and flee!
For well I know, that did great Rustum stand   370
Before thy face this day, and were revealed,
There would be then no talk of fighting more.
But being what I am, I tell thee this,—
Do thou record it in thine inmost soul:
Either thou shalt renounce thy vaunt, and yield,   375
Or else thy bones shall strew this sand, till winds
Bleach them, or Oxus with his summer-floods,
Oxus in summer wash them all away."
  He spoke; and Sohrab answered, on his feet,—

"Art thou so fierce? Thou wilt not fright me so!   380
I am no girl, to be made pale by words.
Yet this thou hast said well, did Rustum stand
Here on this field, there were no fighting then.
But Rustum is far hence, and we stand here.
Begin! thou art more vast, more dread than I;   385
And thou art proved, I know, and I am young,
But yet success sways with the breath of Heaven.
And though thou thinkest that thou knowest sure
Thy victory, yet thou canst not surely know.
For we are all, like swimmers in the sea,   390
Poised on the top of a huge wave of fate,
Which hangs uncertain to which side to fall;
And whether it will heave us up to land,
Or whether it will roll us out to sea,—
Back out to sea, to the deep waves of death,—   395
We know not, and no search will make us know:
Only the event will teach us in its hour."
      He spoke; and Rustum answered not, but hurled
His spear: down from the shoulder, down it came,
As on some partridge in the corn a hawk,   400
That long has towered in the airy clouds,
Drops like a plummet; Sohrab saw it come,
And sprang aside, quick as a flash; the spear
Hissed, and went quivering down into the sand,
Which it sent flying wide. Then Sohrab threw   405
In turn, and full struck Rustum's shield; sharp rang
The iron plates rang sharp, but turned the spear.
And Rustum seized his club, which none but he
Could wield; an unlopped trunk it was, and huge,
Still rough,—like those which men in treeless plains   410
To build them boats fish from the flooded rivers,
Hyphasis or Hydaspes, when, high up
By their dark springs, the wind in winter-time

Hath made in Himalayan forests wrack,
And strewn the channels with torn boughs,—so huge   415
The club which Rustum lifted now, and struck
One stroke; but again Sohrab sprang aside,
Lithe as the glancing snake, and the club came
Thundering to earth, and leapt from Rustum's hand.
And Rustum followed his own blow, and fell   420
To his knees, and with his fingers clutched the sand.
And now might Sohrab have unsheathed his sword,
And pierced the mighty Rustum while he lay
Dizzy, and on his knees, and choked with sand;
But he looked on, and smiled, nor bared his sword,   425
But courteously drew back, and spoke, and said,—
    "Thou strik'st too hard! that club of thine will float
Upon the summer-floods, and not my bones.
But rise, and be not wroth! not wroth am I;
No, when I see thee, wrath forsakes my soul.   430
Thou say'st thou are not Rustum; be it so!
Who art thou, then, that canst so touch my soul?
Boy as I am, I have seen battles too,—
Have waded foremost in their bloody waves,
And heard their hollow roar of dying men;   435
But never was my heart thus touched before.
Are they from Heaven, these softenings of the heart?
O thou old warrior, let us yield to Heaven!
Come, plant we here in earth our angry spears,
And make a truce, and sit upon this sand,   440
And pledge each other in red wine, like friends,
And thou shall talk to me of Rustum's deeds.
There are enough foes in the Persian host,
Whom I may meet, and strike, and feel no pang;
Champions enough Afrasiab has, whom thou   445
May'st fight; fight *them*, when they confront thy spear!
But oh, let there be peace 'twixt thee and me!"

He ceased; but while he spake, Rustum had risen,
And stood erect, trembling with rage; his club
He left to lie, but had regained his spear,   450
Whose fiery point now in his mailed right hand
Blazed bright and baleful, like that autumn-star,
The baleful sign of fevers; dust had soiled
His stately crest, and dimmed his glittering arms.
His breast heaved, his lips foamed, and twice his voice   455
Was choked with rage; at last these words broke way:—
    "Girl! nimble with thy feet, not with thy hands!
Curled minion, dancer, coiner of sweet words!
Fight, let me hear thy hateful voice no more!
Thou art not in Afrasiab's garden now   460
With Tartar girls, with whom thou art wont to dance;
But on the Oxus-sands, and in the dance
Of battle, and with me, who make no play
Of war: I fight it out, and hand to hand.
Speak not to me of truce, and pledge, and wine!   465
Remember all thy valour; try thy feints
And cunning! all the pity I had is gone,
Because thou hast shamed me before both the hosts
With thy light skipping tricks and thy girl's wiles."
    He spoke; and Sohrab kindled at his taunts,   470
And he too drew his sword; at once they rushed
Together, as two eagles on one prey
Come rushing down together from the clouds,
One from the east, one from the west; their shields
Dashed with a clang together, and a din   475
Rose, such as that the sinewy woodcutters
Make often in the forest's heart at morn,
Of hewing axes, crashing trees,—such blows
Rustum and Sohrab on each other hailed.
And you would say that sun and stars took part   480
In that unnatural conflict: for a cloud

Grew suddenly in heaven, and darked the sun
Over the fighters' heads; and a wind rose
Under their feet, and moaning swept the plain,
And in a sandy whirlwind wrapped the pair.   485
In gloom they twain were wrapped, and they alone;
For both the on-looking hosts on either hand
Stood in broad daylight, and the sky was pure,
And the sun sparkled on the Oxus stream.
But in the gloom they fought, with bloodshot eyes   490
And labouring breath. First Rustum struck the shield
Which Sohrab held stiff out; the steel-spiked spear
Rent the tough plates, but failed to reach the skin,
And Rustum plucked it back with angry groan.
Then Sohrab with his sword smote Rustum's helm,   495
Nor clove its steel quite through; but all the crest
He shore away, and that proud horse-hair plume,
Never till now defiled, sank to the dust;
And Rustum bowed his head. But then the gloom
Grew blacker, thunder rumbled in the air   500
And lightnings rent the cloud; and Ruksh the horse,
Who stood at hand, uttered a dreadful cry:
No horse's cry was that, most like the roar
Of some pained desert-lion, who all day
Has trailed the hunter's javelin in his side,   505
And comes at night to die upon the sand;
The two hosts heard that cry, and quaked for fear,
And Oxus curdled as it crossed his stream.
But Sohrab heard, and quailed not, but rushed on,
And struck again; and again Rustum bowed   510
His head; but this time all the blade, like glass,
Sprang in a thousand shivers on the helm,
And in the hand the hilt remained alone.
Then Rustum raised his head; his dreadful eyes
Glared, and he shook on high his menacing spear,   515

And shouted, *Rustum!* Sohrab heard that shout,
And shrank amazed: back he recoiled one step,
And scanned with blinking eyes the advancing form;
And then he stood bewildered, and he dropped
His covering shield, and the spear pierced his side.   520
He reeled, and staggering back sank to the ground.
And then the gloom dispersed, and the wind fell,
And the bright sun broke forth, and melted all
The cloud; and the two armies saw the pair,—
Saw Rustum standing safe upon his feet,   525
And Sohrab wounded on the bloody sand.

   Then, with a bitter smile, Rustum began,—
"Sohrab, thou thoughtest in thy mind to kill
A Persian lord this day, and strip his corpse,
And bear thy trophies to Afrasiab's tent;   530
Or else that the great Rustum would come down
Himself to fight, and that thy wiles would move
His heart to take a gift, and let thee go.
And then that all the Tartar host would praise
Thy courage or thy craft, and spread thy fame,   535
To glad thy father in his weak old age.
Fool, thou art slain, and by an unknown man!
Dearer to the red jackals shalt thou be
Than to thy friends, and to thy father old."

   And, with a fearless mien, Sohrab replied,—   540
"Unknown thou art, yet thy fierce vaunt is vain.
Thou dost not slay me, proud and boastful man!
No! Rustum slays me, and this filial heart.
For, were I matched with ten such men as thee,
And I were that which till to-day I was,   545
They should be lying here, I standing there.
But that belovèd name unnerved my arm,—
That name, and something, I confess, in thee,
Which troubles all my heart, and made my shield

Fall; and thy spear transfixed an unarmed foe.   550
And now thou boastest and insult'st my fate.
But hear thou this, fierce man, tremble to hear:
The mighty Rustum shall avenge my death!
My father, whom I seek through all the world,
He shall avenge my death, and punish thee!"   555
    As when some hunter in the spring hath found
A breeding eagle sitting on her nest,
Upon the craggy isle of a hill-lake,
And pierced her with an arrow as she rose,
And followed her to find her where she fell   560
Far off; anon her mate comes winging back
From hunting, and a great way off descries
His huddling young left sole; at that, he checks
His pinion, and with short uneasy sweeps
Circles above his eyry, with loud screams   565
Chiding his mate back to her nest; but she
Lies dying, with the arrow in her side,
In some far stony gorge out of his ken,
A heap of fluttering feathers,—never more
Shall the lake glass her, flying over it;   570
Never the black and dripping precipices
Echo her stormy scream as she sails by,—
As that poor bird flies home, nor knows his loss,
So Rustum knew not his own loss, but stood
Over his dying son, and knew him not.   575
    And with a cold, incredulous voice, he said,—
"What prate is this of fathers and revenge?
The mighty Rustum never had a son."
    And, with a failing voice, Sohrab replied,—
"Ah, yes, he had! and that lost son am I.   580
Surely the news will one day reach his ear,—
Reach Rustum, where he sits, and tarries long,
Somewhere, I know not where, but far from here;

And pierce him like a stab, and make him leap
To arms, and cry for vengeance upon thee.   585
Fierce man, bethink thee, for an only son!
What will that grief, what will that vengeance, be?
Oh, could I live till I that grief had seen!
Yet him I pity not so much, but her,
My mother, who in Ader-baijan dwells   590
With that old king, her father, who grows grey
With age, and rules over the valiant Koords.
Her most I pity, who no more will see
Sohrab returning from the Tartar camp,
With spoils and honour, when the war is done.   595
But a dark rumour will be bruited up,
From tribe to tribe, until it reach her ear;
And then will that defenceless woman learn
That Sohrab will rejoice her sight no more.
But that in battle with a nameless foe,   600
By the far-distant Oxus, he is slain."
      He spoke; and as he ceased he wept aloud,
Thinking of her he left, and his own death.
He spoke; but Rustum listened, plunged in thought.
Nor did he yet believe it was his son   605
Who spoke, although he called back names he knew;
For he had had sure tidings that the babe
Which was in Ader-baijan born to him
Had been a puny girl, no boy at all—
So that sad mother sent him word, for fear   610
Rustum should seek the boy, to train in arms.
And so he deemed that either Sohrab took,
By a false boast, the style of Rustum's son;
Or that men gave it him, to swell his fame.
So deemed he: yet he listened, plunged in thought;   615
And his soul set to grief, as the vast tide
Of the bright rocking ocean sets to shore

At the full moon; tears gathered in his eyes;
For he remembered his own early youth,
And all its bounding rapture; as at dawn,   620
The shepherd from his mountain-lodge descries
A far, bright city, smitten by the sun,
Through many rolling clouds,—so Rustum saw
His youth; saw Sohrab's mother in her bloom;
And that old king, her father, who loved well   625
His wandering guest, and gave him his fair child
With joy; and all the pleasant life they led,
They three, in that long-distant summer-time,—
The castle, and the dewy woods, and hunt
And hound, and morn on those delightful hills   630
In Ader-baijan. And he saw that youth,
Of age and looks to be his own dear son,
Piteous and lovely, lying on the sand;
Like some rich hyacinth which by the scythe
Of an unskilful gardener has been cut,   635
Mowing the garden grass-plots near its bed,
And lies, a fragrant tower of purple bloom,
On the mown, dying grass,—so Sohrab lay,
Lovely in death, upon the common sand.
And Rustum gazed on him with grief, and said,—   640
    "O Sohrab, thou indeed art such a son
Whom Rustum, wert thou his, might well have loved!
Yet here thou errest, Sohrab, or else men
Have told thee false: thou art not Rustum's son.
For Rustum had no son: one child he had,—   645
But one,—a girl; who with her mother now
Plies some light female task, nor dreams of us,—
Of us she dreams not, nor of wounds, nor war."
    But Sohrab answered him in wrath; for now
The anguish of the deep-fixed spear grew fierce,   650
And he desired to draw forth the steel,

And let the blood flow free, and so to die.
But first he would convince his stubborn foe;
And, rising sternly on one arm, he said,—
    "Man, who art thou who dost deny my words?   655
Truth sits upon the lips of dying men;
And falsehood, while I lived, was far from mine.
I tell thee, pricked upon this arm I bear
That seal which Rustum to my mother gave,
That she might prick it on the babe she bore."   660
    He spoke; and all the blood left Rustum's cheeks,
And his knees tottered, and he smote his hand
Against his breast, his heavy mailèd hand,
That the hard iron corslet clanked aloud;
And to his heart he pressed the other hand,   665
And in a hollow voice he spake, and said,—
    "Sohrab, that were a proof which could not lie!
If thou show this, then art thou Rustum's son."
    Then, with weak hasty fingers, Sohrab loosed
His belt, and near the shoulder bared his arm,   670
And showed a sign in faint vermilion points
Pricked; as a cunning workman, in Pekin,
Pricks with vermilion some clear porcelain vase,
An emperor's gift,—at early morn he paints,
And all day long, and, when night comes, the lamp   675
Lights up his studious forehead and thin hands,—
So delicately pricked the sign appeared
On Sohrab's arm, the sign of Rustum's seal.
It was that griffin which of old reared Zal,
Rustum's great father, whom they left to die,   680
A helpless babe, among the mountain rocks;
Him that kind creature found, and reared, and loved;
Then Rustum took it for his glorious sign.
And Sohrab bared that image on his arm,
And himself scanned it long with mournful eyes,   685

And then he touched it with his hand, and said,—
  "How say'st thou? Is that sign the proper sign
Of Rustum's son, or of some other man's?"
    He spoke; but Rustum gazed, and gazed, and stood
Speechless; and then he uttered one sharp cry,—   690
O boy—thy father! and his voice choked there.
And a dark cloud passed before his eyes,
And his head swam, and he sank down to earth.
But Sohrab crawled to where he lay, and cast
His arms about his neck, and kissed his lips,   695
And with fond faltering fingers stroked his cheeks,
Trying to call him back to life; and life
Came back to Rustum, and he oped his eyes,
And they stood wide with horror; and he seized
In both his hands the dust which lay around,   700
And threw it on his head, and smirched his hair,—
His hair, and face, and beard, and glittering arms;
And strong convulsive groanings shook his breast,
And his sobs choked him; and he clutched his sword,
To draw it, and forever let life out.   705
But Sohrab saw his thought, and held his hands,
And with a soothing voice he spake, and said,—
  "Father, forbear! for I but meet to-day
The doom which at my birth was written down
In Heaven, and thou art Heaven's unconscious hand.   710
Surely my heart cried out that it was thou,
When first I saw thee; and thy heart spoke too,
I know it! But fate trod those promptings down
Under its iron heel; fate, fate engaged
The strife, and hurled me on my father's spear.   715
But let us speak no more of this. I find
My father, let me feel that I have found!
Come, sit beside me on this sand, and take
My head betwixt thy hands, and kiss my cheeks,

68

And wash them with thy tears, and say, *My son!*   720
Quick, quick! for numbered are my sands of life,
And swift; for like the lightning to this field
I came, and like the wind I go away,—
Sudden, and swift, and like a passing wind;
But it was writ in Heaven that this should be."   725
　　So said he; and his voice released the heart
Of Rustum, and his tears broke forth; he cast
His arms round his son's neck, and wept aloud,
And kissed him. And awe fell on both the hosts,
When they saw Rustum's grief; and Ruksh, the horse,   730
With his head bowing to the ground, and mane
Sweeping the dust, came near, and in mute woe
First to the one, then to the other, moved
His head, as if inquiring what their grief
Might mean; and from his dark, compassionate eyes,   735
The big warm tears rolled down, and caked the sand.
But Rustum chid him with stern voice, and said,—
　　"Ruksh, now thou grievest; but, O Ruksh, thy feet
Should then have rotted on their nimble joints,
When first they bore thy master to this field!"   740
　　But Sohrab looked upon the horse, and said,—
"Is this, then, Ruksh? How often, in past days,
My mother told me of thee, thou brave steed,
My terrible father's terrible horse! and said,
That I should one day find thy lord and thee.   745
Come, let me lay my hand upon thy mane!
O Ruksh, thou art more fortunate than I!
For thou hast gone where I shall never go,
And snuffed the breezes of my father's home.
And thou hast trod the sands of Seistan,   750
And seen the River of Helmund, and the Lake
Of Zirrah; and the agèd Zal himself
Has often stroked thy neck, and given thee food,

Corn in a golden platter, soaked with wine,
And said, *O Ruksh! bear Rustum well!* But I 755
Have never known my grandsire's furrowed face,
Nor seen his lofty house in Seistan,
Nor slaked my thirst at the clear Helmund stream,
But lodged among my father's foes, and seen
Afrasiab's cities only, Samarcand, 760
Bokhara, and lone Khiva in the waste,
And the black Toorkmun tents; and only drunk
The desert rivers, Moorghab and Tejend,
Kohik, and where the Kalmuks feed their sheep,
The northern Sir; and this great Oxus stream, 765
The yellow Oxus, by whose brink I die."
        Then, with a heavy groan, Rustum bewailed,—
"Oh that its waves were flowing over me!
Oh that I saw its grains of yellow silt
Roll tumbling in the current o'er my head!" 770
        But, with a grave mild voice, Sohrab replied,—
"Desire not that, my father! thou must live.
For some are born to do great deeds, and live
As some are born to be obscured, and die.
Do thou the deeds I die too young to do, 775
And reap a second glory in thine age;
Thou art my father, and thy gain is mine.
But come! thou seest this great host of men
Which follow me; I pray thee, slay not these!
Let me entreat for them: what have they done? 780
They followed me, my hope, my fame, my star.
Let them all cross the Oxus back in peace.
But me thou must bear hence, not send with them
But carry me with thee to Seistan,
And place me on a bed, and mourn for me,— 785
Thou, and the snow-haired Zal, and all thy friends.
And thou must lay me in that lovely earth,

And heap a stately mound above my bones,
And plant a far-seen pillar over all;
That so the passing horseman on the waste   790
May see my tomb a great way off, and cry,—
Sohrab, the mighty Rustum's son, lies there,
Whom his great father did in ignorance kill!
And I be not forgotten in my grave."
    And with a mournful voice, Rustum replied,—   795
"Fear not! as thou hast said, Sohrab my son,
So shall it be; for I will burn my tents,
And quit the host, and bear thee hence with me,
And carry thee away to Seistan,
And place thee on a bed, and mourn for thee,   800
With the snow-headed Zal, and all my friends.
And I will lay thee in that lovely earth,
And heap a stately mound above thy bones,
And plant a far-seen pillar over all,
And men shall not forget thee in thy grave.   805
And I will spare thy host; yea, let them go!
Let them all cross the Oxus back in peace!
What should I do with slaying any more?
For would that all whom I have ever slain
Might be once more alive,—my bitterest foes,   810
And they who were called champions in their time.
And through whose death I won that fame I have,—
And I were nothing but a common man,
A poor, mean soldier, and without renown,
So thou mightest live too, my son, my son!   815
Or rather would that I, even I myself,
Might now be lying on this bloody sand,
Near death, and by an ignorant stroke of thine,
Not thou of mine! and I might die, not thou;
And I, not thou, be borne to Seistan;   820
And Zal might weep above my grave, not thine;

And say, *O Son, I weep thee not too sore,*
For willingly, I know, thou met'st thine end!
But now in blood and battles was my youth,
And full of blood and battles is my age,   825
And I shall never end this life of blood."
    Then, at the point of death, Sohrab replied,—
"A life of blood indeed, thou dreadful man!
But thou shalt yet have peace: only not now,
Not yet! but thou shalt have it on that day,   830
When thou shalt sail in a high-masted ship,
Thou and the other peers of Kai Khosroo,
Returning home over the salt blue sea,
From laying thy dear master in his grave."
    And Rustum gazed in Sohrab's face, and said,—   835
"Soon be that day, my son, and deep that sea!
Till then, if fate so wills, let me endure."
    He spoke; and Sohrab smiled on him, and took
The spear, and drew it from his side, and eased
His wound's imperious anguish; but the blood   840
Came welling from the open gash, and life
Flowed with the stream; all down his cold white side
The crimson torrent ran, dim now and soiled,
Like the soiled tissue of white violets
Left, freshly gathered, on their native bank,   845
By children whom their nurses call with haste
Indoors from the sun's eye; his head drooped low,
His limbs grew slack; motionless, white, he lay,—
While, with eyes closed; only when heavy gasps,
Deep heavy gasps quivering through all his frame,   850
Convulsed him back to life, he opened them,
And fixed them feebly on his father's face;
Till now all strength was ebbed, and from his limbs
Unwillingly the spirit fled away,
Regretting the warm mansion which it left,   855

And youth, and bloom, and this delightful world.
    So, on the bloody sand, Sohrab lay dead;
And the great Rustum drew his horseman's cloak
Down o'er his face, and sate by his dead son.
As those black granite pillars, once high-reared   860
By Jemshid in Persepolis, to bear
His house, now 'mid their broken flights of steps
Lie prone, enormous, down the mountain side,—
So in the sand lay Rustum by his son.
    And night came down over the solemn waste,   865
And the two gazing hosts, and that sole pair,
And darkened all; and a cold fog, with night,
Crept from the Oxus. Soon a hum arose,
As of a great assembly loosed, and fires
Began to twinkle through the fog; for now   870
Both armies moved to camp, and took their meal;
The Persians took it on the open sands
Southward, the Tartars by the river-marge;
And Rustum and his son were left alone.
    But the majestic river floated on,   875
Out of the mist and hum of that low land,
Into the frosty starlight, and there moved,
Rejoicing, through the hushed Chorasmian waste,
Under the solitary moon; he flowed
Right for the Polar star, past Orgunjè,   880
Brimming, and bright, and large; then sands begin
To hem his watery march, and dam his streams,
And split his currents; that for many a league
The shorn and parcelled Oxus strains along
Through beds of sand and matted rushy isles,—   885
Oxus, forgetting the bright speed he had
In his high mountain cradle in Pamere,
A foiled circuitous wanderer,—till at last
The longed-for dash of waves is heard, and wide

His luminous home of waters opens, bright
And tranquil, from whose floor the new-bathed stars
Emerge, and shine upon the Aral Sea.

    In line 49 of this poem there is what may be called the "inciting" moment; in other words, we are offered a strong clue to the subsequent action:

I seek one man, one man, and one alone—

The foreboding of the tragic outcome of this search is given us in lines 86 through 93, when Peran-Wisa says:

> There go!—Thou wilt not? Yet my heart forebodes
> Danger or death awaits thee on this field.
> Fain would I know thee safe and well, though lost
> To us; fain therefore send thee hence in peace
> To seek thy father, not seek single fights
> In vain. But who can keep the lion's cub
> From ravening, and who govern Rustum's son?
> Go: I will grant thee what thy heart desires."

In these lines we also catch a glimpse of that "tragic flaw," albeit an admirable characteristic, that brings Sohrab to his death: his courage and daring cause him to ignore the advice of an old man who is kindly and wise.

    The epic poet is not limited by the demands of rhyme or stanza form, and so he can be less economical in his use of words than he would have to be with other poetic writing. His pace is leisurely; he has time to create suspense. In so doing, he relies frequently upon the Homeric simile, an elaborate comparison usually beginning with "as when" and ending before the word "so." One of the most famous Homeric similes in literature is in *Sohrab and Rustum*, lines 556 and 573.

    The climax of the poem comes dramatically at line 516, to be followed by a lengthy denouement. The conclusion begins at line 875. Hence we have all the requirements of tragedy, and they are set in the epic tradition.

The role played by the supernatural is expressed most vividly in lines 499 through 515 and in the description of Zal, Rustum's father, who was reared by a griffin. The force of fate is evoked by Sohrab in lines 708 through 725.

3

Narrative Verse

A narrative, whether in prose or verse, describes what happens to a person, animal, place, or thing. The difference between the way a poet and a prose writer tell a story is imposed by the literary medium. The poet has little opportunity for the detailed analysis and description characteristic of the novelist and short-story writer. His *personae* must speak for themselves. When reading a poem, we therefore make deductions from what has been said or done, much as we would at the theater. The result is a more immediate feeling of involvement. We are not mere spectators; we are in a way participants. Our experience can, in a sense, be creative.

Morte d'Arthur, by Alfred, Lord Tennyson (1809–1892), idealizes the king of the Arthurian legend. It is written in blank verse.

Morte d'Arthur

So all day long the noise of battle roll'd
Among the mountains by the winter sea,
Until King Arthur's table, man by man,
Had fallen in Lyonnesse about their lord,

King Arthur; then, because his wound was deep,
The bold Sir Bedivere uplifted him,
Sir Bedivere, the last of all his knights,
And bore him to a chapel nigh the field,
A broken chancel with a broken cross,
That stood on a dark strait of barren land.
On one side lay the ocean, and on one
Lay a great water, and the moon was full.
    Then spake King Arthur to Sir Bedivere:
"The sequel of to-day unsolders all
The goodliest fellowship of famous knights
Whereof this world holds record. Such a sleep
They sleep—the men I loved. I think that we
Shall never more, at any future time,
Delight our souls with talk of knightly deeds.
Walking about the gardens and the halls
Of Camelot, as in the days that were,
I perish by this people which I made,—
Tho' Merlin sware that I should come again
To rule once more—but let what will be be,
I am so deeply smitten thro' the helm
That without help I cannot last till morn.
Thou therefore take my brand Excalibur,
Which was my pride; for thou rememberest how
In those old days, one summer noon, an arm
Rose up from out the bosom of the lake,
Clothed in white samite, mystic, wonderful,
Holding the sword—and how I row'd across
And took it, and have worn it, like a king;
And, wheresoever I am sung or told
In aftertime, this also shall be known.
But now delay not; take Excalibur,
And fling him far into the middle mere;
Watch what thou seest, and lightly bring me word."

To him replied the bold Sir Bedivere:
"It is not meet, Sir King, to leave thee thus,
Aidless, alone, and smitten thro' the helm.
A little thing may harm a wounded man.
Yet I thy hest will all perform at full,
Watch what I see, and lightly bring thee word."
So saying, from the ruin'd shrine he stept
And in the moon athwart the place of tombs,
Where lay the mighty bones of ancient men,
Old knights, and over them the sea-wind sang
Shrill, chill, with flakes of foam. He, stepping down
By zigzag paths and juts of pointed rock,
Came on the shining levels of the lake.
There drew he forth the brand Excalibur,
And o'er him, drawing it, the winter moon,
Brightening the skirts of a long cloud, ran forth
And sparkled keen with frost against the hilt;
For all the haft twinkled with diamond sparks,
Myriads of topaz-lights, and jacinth work
Of subtlest jewellery. He gazed so long
That both his eyes were dazzled, as he stood,
This way and that dividing the swift mind,
In act to throw; but at the last it seem'd
Better to leave Excalibur conceal'd
There in the many-knotted water-flags,
That whistled stiff and dry about the marge.
So strode he back slow to the wounded king.
Then spake King Arthur to Sir Bedivere:
"Hast thou perform'd my mission which I gave?
What is it thou hast seen, or what hast heard?"
And answer made the bold Sir Bedivere:
"I heard the ripple washing in the reeds,
And the wild water lapping on the crag."
To whom replied King Arthur, faint and pale:

"Thou hast betray'd thy nature and thy name,
Not rendering true answer, as beseem'd
Thy fealty, nor like a noble knight;
For surer sign had follow'd, either hand,
Or voice, or else a motion of the mere.
This is a shameful thing for men to lie.
Yet now, I charge thee, quickly go again
As thou art lief and dear, and do the thing
I bade thee, watch, and lightly bring me word."
    Then went Sir Bedivere the second time
Across the ridge, and paced beside the mere,
Counting the dewy pebbles, fix'd in thought;
But when he saw the wonder of the hilt,
How curiously and strangely chased, he smote
His palms together, and he cried aloud:
    "And if indeed I cast the brand away,
Surely a precious thing, one worthy note,
Should thus be lost forever from the earth,
Which might have pleased the eyes of many men.
What good should follow this, if this were done?
What harm, undone? deep harm to disobey,
Seeing obedience is the bond of rule.
Were it well to obey then, if a king demand
An act unprofitable, against himself?
The king is sick, and knows not what he does.
What record, or what relic of my lord
Should be to aftertime, but empty breath
And rumours of a doubt? but were this kept,
Stored in some treasure-house of mighty kings,
Some one might show it at a joust of arms,
Saying, 'King Arthur's sword, Excalibur,
Wrought by the lonely maiden of the lake;
Nine years she wrought it, sitting in the deeps
Upon the hidden bases of the hills.'

So might some old man speak in the aftertime
To all the people, winning reverence;
But now much honour and much fame were lost."
    So spake he, clouded with his own conceit,
And hid Excalibur the second time,
And so strode back slow to the wounded king.
    Then spoke King Arthur, breathing heavily:
"What is it thou hast seen, or what hast heard?"
    And answer made the bold Sir Bedivere:
"I heard the water lapping on the crag,
And the long ripple washing in the reeds."
    To whom replied King Arthur, much in wrath:
"Ah, miserable and unkind, untrue,
Unknightly, traitor-hearted! Woe is me!
Authority forgets a dying king,
Laid widow'd of the power in his eyes
That bow'd the will. I see thee what thou art,
For thou, the latest-left of all my knights,
In whom should meet the offices of all,
Thou wouldst betray me for the precious hilt;
Either from lust of gold, or like a girl
Valuing the giddy pleasure of the eyes.
Yet, for a man may fail in duty twice,
And the third time may prosper, get thee hence;
But, if thou spare to fling Excalibur,
I will arise and slay thee with my hands."
    Then quickly rose Sir Bedivere, and ran,
And, leaping down the ridges lightly, plunged
Among the bulrush-beds, and clutch'd the sword,
And strongly wheel'd and threw it. The great brand
Made lightnings in the splendour of the moon.
And flashing round and round, and whirl'd in an arch,
Shot like a streamer of the northern morn,
Seen where the moving isles of winter shock

By night, with noises of the northern sea,
So flash'd and fell the brand Excalibur;
But ere he dipped the surface, rose an arm
Cloth'd in white samite, mystic, wonderful,
And caught him by the hilt, and brandish'd him
Three times, and drew him under in the mere.
And lightly went the other to the king.
    Then spoke King Arthur, drawing thicker breath:
"Now see I by thine eyes that this is done.
Speak out; what is it thou hast heard, or seen?"
    And answer made the bold Sir Bedivere:
"Sir King, I closed mine eyelids, lest the gems
Should blind my purpose, for I never saw—
Nor shall see, here or elsewhere, till I die,
Not tho' I live three lives of mortal men,
So great a miracle as yonder hilt.
Then with both hands I flung him, wheeling him;
But when I look'd again, behold an arm,
Clothed in white samite, mystic, wonderful,
That caught him by the hilt, and brandish'd him
Three times, and drew him under in the mere."
    And answer made King Arthur, breathing hard:
"My end draws nigh; 'tis time that I were gone.
Make broad thy shoulders to receive my weight.
And bear me to the margin; yet I fear
My wound hath taken cold, and I shall die."
    So saying, from the pavement he half rose,
Slowly, with pain, reclining on his arm,
And looking wistfully with wide blue eyes
As in a picture. Him Sir Bedivere
Remorsefully regarded thro' his tears,
And would have spoken, but he found not words,
Then took with care, and kneeling on one knee,
O'er both his shoulders drew the languid hands,

And rising bore him thro' the place of tombs.
    But, as he walk'd, King Arthur panted hard,
Like one that feels a nightmare on his bed
When all the house is mute. So sigh'd the king,
Muttering and murmuring at his ear, "Quick, quick!
I fear it is too late, and I shall die."
But the other swiftly strode from ridge to ridge,
Clothed with his breath, and looking, as he walk'd,
Larger than human on the frozen hills.
He heard the deep behind him, and a cry
Before. His own thought drove him like a goad.
Dry clash'd his harness in the icy caves
And barren chasms, and all to left and right
The bare black cliff clang'd round him, as he based
His feet on juts of slippery crag that rang
Sharp-smitten with the dint of armed heels—
And on a sudden, lo! the level lake,
And the long glories of the winter moon.
    Then saw they how there hove a dusky barge,
Dark as a funeral scarf from stern to stern,
Beneath them; and descending they were ware
That all the decks were dense with stately forms
Black-stoled, black-hooded, like a dream—by these
Three queens with crowns of gold—and from them rose
A cry that shiver'd to the tingling stars,
And, as it were one voice, an agony
Of lamentation, like a wind that shrills
All night in a waste land, where no one comes,
Or hath come, since the making of the world.
    Then murmur'd Arthur, "Place me in the barge,"
And to the barge they came. There those three queens
Put forth their hands, and took the king, and wept.
But she that rose the tallest of them all

And fairest, laid his head upon her lap,
And loosed the shatter'd casque, and chafed his hands,
And call'd him by his name, complaining loud,
And dropping bitter tears against his brow
Striped with dark blood; for all his face was white
And colourless, and like the wither'd moon
Smote by the fresh beam of the springing east;
And all his greaves and cuisses dash'd with drops
Of onset; and the light and lustrous curls—
That made his forehead like a rising sun
High from the dais-throne—were parch'd with dust;
Or, clotted into points and hanging loose,
Mix'd with the knightly growth that fringed his lips.
So like a shatter'd column lay the king;
Not like that Arthur who, with lance in rest,
From spur to plume a star of tournament,
Shot thro' the lists at Camelot, and charged
Before the eyes of ladies and of kings.
    Then loudly cried the bold Sir Bedivere:
"Ah! my Lord Arthur, whither shall I go?
Where shall I hide my forehead and my eyes?
For now I see the true old times are dead,
When every morning brought a noble chance,
And every chance brought out a noble knight.
Such times have been not since the light that led
The Holy Elders with the gift of myrrh.
But now the whole ROUND TABLE is dissolved
Which was an image of the mighty world;
And I, the last, go forth companionless,
And the days darken round me, and the years,
Among new men, strange faces, other minds."
    And slowly answer'd Arthur from the barge:
"The old order changeth, yielding place to new,

And God fulfils himself in many ways,
Lest one good custom should corrupt the world.
Comfort thyself: what comfort is in me?
I have lived my life, and that which I have done
May He within himself make pure! but thou,
If thou shouldst never see my face again,
Pray for my soul. More things are wrought by prayer
Than this world dreams of. Wherefore, let thy voice
Rise like a fountain for me night and day.
For what are men better than sheep or goats
That nourish a blind life within the brain,
If, knowing God, they lift not hands of prayer
Both for themselves and those who call them friend?
For so the whole round earth is every way
Bound by gold chains about the feet of God.
But now farewell. I am going a long way
With these thou seest—if indeed I go—
For all my mind is clouded with a doubt—
To the island-valley of Avilion;
Where falls not hail, or rain, or any snow,
Nor ever wind blows loudly, but it lies
Deep-meadow'd, happy, fair with orchard lawns
And bowery hollows crown'd with summer sea,
Where I will heal me of my grievous wound."
    So said he, and the barge with oar and sail
Moved from the brink, like some full-breasted swan
That, fluting a wild carol ere her death,
Ruffles her pure cold plume, and takes the flood
With swarthy webs. Long stood Sir Bedivere
Revolving many memories, till the hull
Look'd one black dot against the verge of dawn,
And on the mere the wailing died away.

The slow pace and majestic lines of this poem result from the use of many monosyllables, with each word receiving its due stress. Instead of riding above the narrative, alliteration and assonance combine closely with sense. Detail is precise and pictorial; sounds are descriptive in themselves.

Dramatic Verse

Narrative verse can also be dramatic; "My Last Duchess," by Robert Browning (1812–1889), is a good example of dramatic monologue.

My Last Duchess

FERRARA

That's my last Duchess painted on the wall,
Looking as if she were alive. I call
That piece a wonder, now: Frà Pandolf's hands
Worked busily a day, and there she stands.
Will't please you sit and look at her? I said
"Frà Pandolf" by design, for never read
Strangers like you that pictured countenance,
The depth and passion of its earnest glance,
But to myself they turned (since none puts by
The curtain I have drawn for you, but I)
And seemed as they would ask me, if they durst,
How such a glance came there; so, not the first
Are you to turn and ask thus. Sir, 'twas not
Her husband's presence only, called that spot
Of joy into the Duchess' cheek: perhaps
Frà Pandolf chanced to say "Her mantle laps

Over my lady's wrist too much," or "Paint
Must never hope to reproduce the faint
Half-flush that dies along her throat:" such stuff
Was courtesy, she thought, and cause enough
For calling up that spot of joy. She had
A heart—how shall I say?—too soon made glad,
Too easily impressed; she liked whate'er
She looked on, and her looks went everywhere.
Sir, 'twas all one! My favour at her breast,
The dropping of the daylight in the West,
The bough of cherries some officious fool
Broke in the orchard for her, the white mule
She rode with round the terrace—all and each
Would draw from her alike the approving speech,
Or blush, at least. She thanked men—good! but thanked
Somehow—I know not how—as if she ranked
My gift of a nine-hundred-years-old name
With anybody's gift. Who'd stoop to blame
This sort of trifling? Even had you skill
In speech—(which I have not)—to make your will
Quite clear to such an one, and say, "Just this
Or that in you disgusts me; here you miss,
Or there exceed the mark"—and if she let
Herself be lessoned so, nor plainly set
Her wits to yours, forsooth, and made excuse,
—E'en then would be some stooping; and I choose
Never to stoop. Oh sir, she smiled, no doubt,
Whene'er I passed her; but who passed without
Much the same smile? This grew; I gave commands;
Then all smiles stopped together. There she stands
As if alive. Will't please you rise? We'll meet
The company below, then. I repeat,
The Count your master's known munificence

Is ample warrant that no just pretence
Of mine for dowry will be disallowed;
Though his fair daughter's self, as I avowed
At starting, is my object. Nay, we'll go
Together down, sir. Notice Neptune, though,
Taming a sea-horse, thought a rarity,
Which Claus of Innsbruck cast in bronze for me!

Browning makes use of the dramatic monologue form extensively and brilliantly in his poetic works, and in this particular poem achieves a remarkable *tour de force*.

As the curtain rises, the Duke of Ferrara is speaking with the emissary of an unnamed count about his impending marriage with the count's daughter (actually it is not until the last eight lines of the poem that we find this out). He is showing his guest around his art gallery, with a kind of obnoxious cordiality, and it soon becomes apparent that he collects women as well as works of art. The poem is a reflection of Browning's feeling for Italy, of his interest in the Renaissance period in general and the grotesque in particular; all the aestheticism, the love of beautiful possessions that characterize the Renaissance are personified in the Duke. He points out a painting—a portrait of his last wife—and from his manner and his language we feel he sees little difference between a wife and one of the paintings or pieces of sculpture in his collection.

Certainly the Duke is garrulous, yet it is his manner that suggests subtlety and craftiness. He relies upon innuendo and insinuation and is a master of understatement. His speech is direct only when his thoughts reach a climax, and thus at such moments he is able to give his words an added emphasis.

"My Last Duchess" is written in rhymed couplets, but the poet cleverly uses "enjambment" (running on of lines), and by doing so relieves the pairs of rhyming lines of monotony.

The "Old Chestnut"

A great German poet, Johann Wolfgang von Goethe (1749–1832), once said that "art is bounded without and boundless within." By this he meant that a work of art must be contained within certain limitations while treating of a limitless theme. For example, a painting must be executed within the bounds—that is, the limitations—of a canvas; a sonnet too must be of a particular length, meter, and rhyme scheme. Yet within this prescribed framework, the work of art must contain thoughts and feelings so significant that we find with each reappraisal new illumination and excitement.

If we begin to take a work of art for granted, if we are deprived of a sense of growth, of the extended pleasure a good poem should bring us, something must surely be wrong. At this point we may well feel that even its initial impact on us was questionable; perhaps we feel cheated. Yet it is only by reading and rereading poetry that our critical faculty can be sharpened, so that in time we can judge for ourselves just what constitutes a good poem.

When we refer to a poem as an "old chestnut," we usually mean that the work has become so well known to us that it fails to evoke any further response. It follows that we approach it uncritically, although it is always possible that the dust that has been allowed to settle on it has only temporarily obscured its true nature. Because we have liked this poem in the past, however, we may on occasion turn back to it and others like it simply because they are familiar. Sometimes this can be rewarding.

And so we come to "The Raven," by Edgar Allan Poe (1809–1849). Most of us feel a certain affection for this poem, and with good reason, for it excels in creating an atmosphere of mystery, and its lugubrious refrain has undoubted dramatic force.

But inevitably there comes a time when a rereading of "The Raven" may pall, when it may no longer seem "bounded without and boundless within."

The Raven

Once upon a midnight dreary, while I pondered, weak and
      weary,
Over many a quaint and curious volume of forgotten lore—
While I nodded, nearly napping, suddenly there came a tapping,
As of some one gently rapping, rapping at my chamber door.
" 'Tis some visitor," I muttered, "tapping at my chamber door—
      Only this and nothing more."

Ah, distinctly I remember it was in the bleak December;
And each separate dying ember wrought its ghost upon the
      floor.
Eagerly I wished the morrow;—vainly I had sought to borrow
From my books surcease of sorrow—sorrow for the lost Lenore—
For the rare and radiant maiden whom the angels name Lenore—
      Nameless *here* for evermore.

And the silken, sad, uncertain rustling of each purple curtain
Thrilled me—filled me with fantastic terrors never felt before;
So that now, to still the beating of my heart, I stood repeating
" 'Tis some visitor entreating entrance at my chamber door—
Some late visitor entreating entrance at my chamber door;—
      This it is and nothing more."

Presently my soul grew stronger; hesitating then no longer,
"Sir," said I, "or Madam, truly your forgiveness I implore;
But the fact is I was napping, and so gently you came rapping,
And so faintly you came tapping, tapping at my chamber door,
That I scarce was sure I heard you"—here I open wide the door;
      Darkness there and nothing more.

Deep into that darkness peering, I stood there wondering, fearing,
Doubting, dreaming dreams no mortal ever dared to dream
    before;
But the silence was unbroken, and the stillness gave no token,
And the only word there spoken was the whispered word,
    "Lenore!"
This I whispered, and an echo murmured back the word
    "Lenore!"
      Merely this and nothing more.

Back into the chamber turning, all my soul within me burning.
Soon again I heard a tapping somewhat louder than before.
"Surely," said I, "surely that is something at my window lattice;
Let me see, then, what thereat is, and this mystery explore—
Let my heart be still a moment and this mystery explore;—
      'Tis the wind and nothing more!"

Open here I flung the shutter, when, with many a flirt and
    flutter
In there stepped a stately Raven of the saintly days of yore.
Not the least obeisance made he; not a minute stopped or stayed
    he;
But, with mien of lord or lady, perched above my chamber
    door—
Perched upon a bust of Pallas just above my chamber door—
      Perched, and sat, and nothing more.

Then this ebony bird beguiling my sad fancy into smiling,
By the grave and stern decorum of the countenance it wore,
"Though thy crest be shorn and shaven, thou," I said, "art sure
    no craven,
Ghostly grim and ancient Raven wandering from the Nightly
    shore—
Tell me what thy lordly name is on the Night's Plutonian shore!"
      Quoth the Raven, "Nevermore."

Much I marveled this ungainly fowl to hear discourse so plainly,
Though its answer little meaning—little relevancy bore;
For we cannot help agreeing that no living human being
Ever yet was blessed with seeing bird above his chamber door—
Bird or beast upon the sculptured bust above his chamber door,
    With such name as "Nevermore."

But the Raven, sitting lonely on the placid bust, spoke only
That one word, as if his soul in that one word he did outpour.
Nothing further then he uttered—not a feather then he fluttered—
Till I scarcely more than muttered "Other friends have flown
    before—
On the morrow *he* will leave me, as my hopes have flown before."
    Then the bird said "Nevermore."

Startled at the stillness broken by reply so aptly spoken,
"Doubtless," said I, "what it utters is its only stock and store
Caught from some unhappy master whom unmerciful Disaster
Followed fast and followed faster till his songs one burden bore—
Till the dirges of his Hope that melancholy burden bore
    Of 'Never—nevermore.' "

But the Raven still beguiling all my fancy into smiling,
Straight I wheeled a cushioned seat in front of bird, and bust and
    door;
Then, upon the velvet sinking, I betook myself to linking
Fancy unto fancy, thinking what this ominous bird of yore—
What this grim, ungainly, ghastly, gaunt and ominous bird of
    yore
    Meant in croaking "Nevermore."

This I sat engaged in guessing, but no syllable expressing
To the fowl whose fiery eyes now burned into my bosom's core;
This and more I sat divining, with my head at ease reclining
On the cushion's velvet lining that the lamp-light gloated o'er,
But whose velvet lining with the lamp-light gloating o'er,
    She shall press, ah, nevermore!

Then, methought, the air grew denser, perfumed from an unseen
      censer
Swung by Seraphim whose foot-falls tinkled on the tufted floor.
"Wretch," I cried, "thy God hath lent thee—by these angels
      he hath sent thee
Respite—respite and nepenthe from thy memories of Lenore;
Quaff, oh quaff this kind nepenthe and forget this lost Lenore!"
    Quoth the Raven "Nevermore."

"Prophet!" said I, "thing of evil! prophet still, if bird or devil!—
Whether Tempter sent, or whether tempest tossed thee here
      ashore,
Desolate yet all undaunted, on this desert land enchanted—
On this home by Horror haunted—tell me truly, I implore—
Is there—*is* there balm in Gilead?—tell me—tell me, I implore!"
    Quoth the Raven "Nevermore."

"Prophet!" said I, "thing of evil!—prophet still, if bird or devil!
By that Heaven that bends above us—by that God we both
      adore—
Tell this soul with sorrow laden if, within the distant Aidenn,
It shall clasp a sainted maiden whom the angels name Lenore—
Clasp a rare and radiant maiden whom the angels name Lenore."
    Quoth the Raven "Nevermore."

"Be that word our sign of parting, bird or fiend!" I shrieked,
        up-starting—
"Get thee back into the tempest and the Night's Plutonian shore!
Leave no black plume as a token of that lie thy soul hath spoken!
Leave my loneliness unbroken!—quit the bust above my door!
Take thy beak from out my heart, and take thy form from off
        my door!"
            Quoth the Raven "Nevermore."

And the Raven, never flitting, still is sitting, *still* is sitting
On the pallid bust of Pallas just above my chamber door;
And his eyes have all the seeming of a demon's that is dreaming,
And the lamp-light o'er him streaming throws his shadow on the
        floor;
And my soul from out that shadow that lies floating on the floor
        Shall be lifted—nevermore!

Because of the demands of rhyme and rhythm, poets take
certain liberties known as "poetic license." To be overcritical of
these liberties is to be pedantic and fussy, yet one finds little
justification for rhyming "lattice" with "thereat is." And although
there may be some justification in the sound symbolism of "flirt"
and "flutter," to suggest the movement of the raven, the words
are not appropriate to the solemn mood of the poem. And what is
the sense of "with mien of lord or lady" when the poet has just
referred to the bird with a masculine pronoun?

It would serve very little purpose to continue with examples
of Poe's abuse of poetic license. We can rest our case for the
need to observe the sometimes very necessary restrictions of
form.

An even more serious doubt arises when we think about the
content of "The Raven." Is it "boundless within"? Does it really
say anything significant, and is it illuminating to the reader? The
poet does not even tell us how this very knowing raven came by

his extraordinary powers of insight. Is it enough to create an atmosphere of mystery? Without a drama of significance being unfolded against it, we are left with little more than a stageset.

You may well wonder why, if it has such pronounced deficiencies, "The Raven," should enjoy the popularity it has for such a long time. One of the reasons is its resounding and effective rhythm and the melodrama it suggests. But such attractions are surface qualities and cannot long satisfy.

4

Imagery and the English Sonnet

The sonnet, like almost all English verse forms, did not originate in England, but was borrowed from a foreign country and adapted to our tongue. It is thought to have originated in Provence and traveled to Italy, from whence it was introduced into the English language. One of the most complex of all verse forms, the sonnet is made up of fourteen lines of iambic pentameter, with a prescribed rhyme scheme and expressing a single thought. It is the rhyme scheme that determines the particular form—English or Italian, with their variations.

Before, however, we concern ourselves more specifically with the structure and content of our selected sonnets, let us think for a moment about imagery; for it is within the exacting structure of the sonnet that we find many of the most beautiful images in our language.

We can say that "imagery is the mental reproduction of sense perception," but this is a rather meaningless jumble of words until we stop to consider them carefully. We know that ideas come to us through our senses. We touch, taste, smell, hear, or see something, and through nerves and mental processes our experience is refined into thought.

Let us try an experiment. Think, for example, of a steak cooking over charcoal—something all of you, I hope, have observed. The first thing you do in your imagination is to see it—thick, red, well-marbled with fat. If the coals are right, you will presently hear the hissing of fat followed by a delectable smell. And if the cook knows what he or she is doing, in a matter of minutes you will feel the steak against your lips and taste its delicious substance. But at this point the steak is not in fact here for you to enjoy, and all the writing in the world cannot create the same experience as eating one. Perhaps we can say, however, that reading or hearing about a steak is the next best thing to eating one.

Now you have seen, at a somewhat unpoetic level, how one can reproduce sense perception in one's mind. Mentally you saw, heard, smelled, tasted, and even felt a steak. The poetic image is not quite so obvious, but it works the same way.

Besides its appeal to the senses, the image is frequently symbolic—that is, it stands for something different from itself. Usually it is presented through figurative language.

Because the sonneteer is confined to just so many syllables to a line and just so many lines to a poem, he must say much in a little. One of his chief devices for this purpose is the image.

The English Sonnet

The English sonnet was brought to its perfection by William Shakespeare (1564–1616), and thus "Shakespearean" is synonymous with "English" when we are referring to sonnets. The Shakespearean sonnet rhymes *a b a b c d c d e f e f g g*. The major divisions are, therefore, three quatrains, each expressing, usually figuratively, a different aspect of the theme of the sonnet, and a concluding couplet, in which the poet summarizes or restates his fundamental thought.

Sonnet 73 in the opinion of many is the "apotheosis," or highest development, of the Shakespearean sonnet.

Sonnet 73

That time of year thou may'st in me behold
When yellow leaves, or none, or few, do hang
Upon those boughs which shake against the cold,
Bare ruin'd choirs where late the sweet birds sang.
In me thou see'st the twilight of such day
As after sunset fadeth in the west,
Which by and by black night doth take away,
Death's second self, that seals up all in rest.
In me thou see'st the glowing of such fire
That on the ashes of his youth doth lie,
As the death-bed whereon it must expire,
Consum'd with that which it was nourish'd by.
This thou perceiv'st, which makes thy love more strong,
To love that well which thou must leave ere long.

The first four lines of this sonnet obviously refer to the fall of the year—not quite winter, but late fall. Observe those boughs which, like people, "shake against the cold." Suddenly they are no longer people; they have assumed the appearance of the exposed rafters and beams of a church whose choir, the area before the chancel where the choristers sit, has been laid bare by decrepitude. The choir, or birds, no longer sing in the ruined church, or bare trees. This entire scene, elaborate in detail, is an image evoked by only ten syllables:

Bare ruin'd choirs, where late the sweet birds sang. . . .

But the image is not entirely visual. The birds' former singing—it diminishes as autumn advances—gives us an "auditory image." In addition, we can feel the chill of the late fall air and the desolation of a ruin.

What thought is being conveyed by the symbols in the first four lines? It is that the poet is middle-aged; he is in the autumn of his life.

In the second quatrain the poet expresses the same idea, but with a new image—sunset, which is to the day what autumn is to the year. Sunset leads into night, and night brings sleep; sleep almost like death, "death's second self." Fading day, fading life, the fading year—we *see* these, but we also *feel* the chill of dark.

The final quatrain gives us a third variation on the same thought. This time the image is tactile rather than visual. To be sure, we see a fire, but it is what we feel from it that concerns us most. This final image is a bit more complex than the preceding two because it presents a paradox, or an apparent contradiction which is nonetheless true. Youth is both fire and vigor, and yet that very fire and vigor are the cause of their own destruction. It is only when a fire has burned to ashes that it has served its purpose. In *Macbeth* Shakespeare touches on the same idea with a similar image when he says of life, "Out, out, brief candle!" As soon as candles or fires begin to live, so also do they begin to die.

Finally, in the concluding couplet, the basic theme of the sonnet is succinctly expressed in direct language. Through an awareness of the approach and inevitability of death, that most compelling of human emotions, love, remains.

"High Flight," written by a little-known Canadian poet, John G. Magee, Jr. (1922–1941), follows the general form of the English, or Shakespearean sonnet, although it takes liberties with the rhyme scheme. It is the work of a poet who died before his twentieth birthday, and it is youthful and vigorous in feeling. This effect is achieved in part because many of the words in the poem are verbs or verbals.

High Flight[1]

Oh! I have slipped the surly bonds of earth
And danced the skies on laughter-silvered wings;
Sunward I've climbed, and joined the tumbling mirth
Of sun-split clouds—and done a hundred things
You have not dreamed of—wheeled and soared and swung
High in the sunlit silence. Hovering there
I've chased the shouting wind along, and flung
My eager craft through footless halls of air.
Up, up the long, delirious, burning blue
I've topped the wind-swept heights with easy grace,
Where never lark, nor even eagle flew—
And, while with silent, lifting mind I've trod
The high untrespassed sanctity of space,
Put out my hand and touched the face of God.

The Italian Sonnet

Like the English sonnet, named after Shakespeare, who perfected
the form, the Italian is frequently called Petrarchan, after the
poet Francesco Petrarch. He lived in Italy from 1304 to 1374. The
rhyme scheme of this type of poem is divided into two distinct
parts: the first eight lines, or "octave," rhyme *a b b a a b b a;* the
final six lines (a sonnet is always of fourteen lines in length) or
"sestet," have a *c d c d c d* rhyming pattern or some variation of
it. But the theme of the sonnet comes in the opening four lines,
or quatrain, and is developed in the next four. It is reflected again
in the "tercet," as the first three lines of the sestet are called; the
final tercet brings the work to an emphatic close.

[1] By Pilot-Officer John Gillespie Magee, Jr., RCAF.

The story goes that when for the first time the English poet John Keats (1795–1821) was shown a 1616 folio of George Chapman's translation of Homer, he and a friend stayed up all night reading it. The next morning Keats wrote his famous sonnet, "On First Looking into Chapman's Homer," a magnificent work that contradicts its somewhat prosaic title. It is Petrarchan in form, as are the two poems that follow it.

On First Looking into Chapman's Homer

Much have I travell'd in the realms of gold,
And many goodly states and kingdoms seen;
Round many western islands have I been
Which bards in fealty to Apollo hold.
Oft of one wide expanse had I been told
That deep-brow'd Homer ruled as his demesne;
Yet did I never breathe its pure serene
Till I heard Chapman speak out loud and bold:
Then felt I like some watcher of the skies
When a new planet swims into his ken;
Or like stout Cortez when with eagle eyes
He star'd at the Pacific—and all his men
Look'd at each other with a wild surmise—
Silent, upon a peak in Darien.

Few sonnets illustrate better the special sights and insights a poet possesses. Keats's view is not a detailed analysis or description; it is a concentrated expression of his experience. What he describes is a soaring voyage of discovery; and this is an image that is central in the poem.

The next example of a Petrarchan sonnet, "Composed upon Westminster Bridge," is also by an English poet, William Wordsworth (1770–1850).

Composed upon Westminster Bridge
Sept. 3, 1802

Earth has not anything to show more fair:
    Dull would he be of soul who could pass by
    A sight so touching in its majesty:
This City now doth like a garment wear
The beauty of the morning; silent, bare,
    Ships, towers, domes, theaters, and temples lie
    Open unto the fields, and to the sky;
All bright and glittering in the smokeless air.
Never did sun more beautifully steep
    In his first splendour valley, rock, or hill;
Ne'er saw I, never felt, a calm so deep!
    The river glideth at his own sweet will:
Dear God! the very houses seem asleep;
    And all that mighty heart is lying still!

So apt is the poet's imagery that the reader is part of the stillness of early morning in London. In the view of the city that the poem describes the only movement is that of the river that "glideth at his own sweet will." We too feel calm and hushed.

The next sonnet, by Edna St. Vincent Millay (1892–1950), is also Petrarchan; and even though it was written comparatively recently—in this century—it observes all the conventions of the early sonnet form. But the rhyme scheme of the sestet (the last six of the fourteen lines in the poem) is not the same as that of the two preceding works. As you can see, the pattern is *c d d c c d*.

Euclid Alone Has Looked on Beauty Bare[2]

Euclid alone has looked on Beauty bare.
Let all who prate of Beauty hold their peace,
And lay them prone upon the earth and cease
To ponder on themselves, the while they stare
At nothing, intricately drawn nowhere
In shapes of shifting lineage; let geese
Gabble and hiss, but heroes seek release
From dusty bondage into luminous air.

O blinding hour, O holy, terrible day,
When first the shaft into his vision shone
Of light anatomized! Euclid alone
Has looked on Beauty bare. Fortunate they
Who, though once only and then but far away,
Have heard her massive sandal set on stone.

5

Lyric Verse

Sometimes it is tempting to think more about the poet than about his work, especially if he has a vivid personality or has led an unusual or fascinating life. This temptation is strong when it comes to John Donne (1573–1631), who seems to have been two entirely different people. As a young man he was witty, cynical, impulsive, and urbane; after the age of forty, when he took orders (eventually becoming Dean of St. Paul's), he was pious, wise, and humanitarian. His early works are worldly, secular, and even erotic; most of them were love poems. Much of his later work is prose, and almost all of it is of a deeply religious nature. It was during this second period in Donne's life that he wrote his "Devotions upon Emergent Occasions" (1623), of which the most famous is Number 17. It was from this work that Ernest Hemingway chose the title of his novel *For Whom the Bell Tolls*.

Donne is preeminent among those late sixteenth- and early seventeenth-century poets who, a century later, were styled "metaphysical" by Dr. Johnson, the great critic and lexicographer. The term is used because the writings of these poets frequently contain elaborate figures of speech employing unusual, and often paradoxical, images, learned allusions, and subtle argumentation, in an attempt to relate spiritual man to the physical universe.

Whenever there is a serious discussion of poetry, the words "tone" and "mood" are almost always heard. They are not difficult terms, but they must be clearly understood and differentiated. The writer's choice of words, his rhythms, stanza forms, and his figurative language—all help determine the tone of his work. Tone conveys the poet's own attitude toward what he is writing and toward his reader; is he, the poet, serious, or is he being light and amusing? Ultimately, perhaps, one might need to know how the poet's voice would sound were he reading the poem aloud. Mood, too, is as personal and subjective, since it encompasses the emotional atmosphere created by the work. Does it make you happy, or does it make you sad? Does it engender disgust or sympathy?

The tone of Donne's poem that we have selected is cynical—another word demanding thorough understanding. (A cynic doubts the motives of others; he has a sneering disbelief in sincerity and noble behavior.) It is a lyric, written during the poet's early, secular period, and it is in the form of a plea—would someone find a woman both "true and fair" for him? Today usually referred to as "Go and Catch a Falling Star," Donne himself entitled it "Song."

Song

Go and catch a falling star,
  Get with child a mandrake root,
Tell me where all past years are,
  Or who cleft the Devil's foot,
Teach me to hear mermaids' singing,
  Or to keep off envy's stinging,
    And find
    What wind
Serves to advance an honest mind.

If thou be'st born to strange sights,
   Things invisible to see,
Ride ten thousand days and nights,
   Till age snow white hairs on thee;
Thou, when thou return'st, will tell me
All strange wonders that befell thee,
    And swear
    No where
Lives a woman true and fair.

If thou find'st one, let me know,
   Such a pilgrimage were sweet.
Yet do not, I would not go,
   Though at next door we might meet.
Though she were true when you met her,
And last, till you write your letter,
    Yet she
    Will be
False, ere I come, to two, or three.

    The poem begins on a peculiarly perverse note, as though to say: "Go and do the impossible for me. Hold your hat out and catch a meteor!" The second line establishes the tone by alluding to one of the many curious superstitions connected with the mandrake root, which was thought to resemble the human body. The coarseness of this line underscores the poet's cynicism. He continues to taunt by referring to other ludicrous but widely accepted beliefs. But if it reads like banter at its opening, at the conclusion of the stanza there is a serious and bitter thought: honesty, says the poet, is ephemeral, borne on the air, transient. After reading the rest of the poem, we assume that what Donne is describing here is the question of women's honesty or fidelity.

Observe how he puts on the brakes and changes gear from the trochaic tetrameter of the first six lines to the iambic monometer of lines seven and eight. The poet's change of pace gives skillful emphasis to the final thought of the stanza.

The second stanza, following the same rhythmic pattern as the first, refers once more to the supernatural—that which cannot be explained by known laws and is seen only by those with psychic powers. The poet's cynicism has thus reached a new intensity and implies a profound distrust of women.

In the final stanza, again in the same metrical form, the poet gives full vent to his rage and bitterness and bluntly says what he means. But think about the word "pilgrimage" in the second line. Usually, one goes on a pilgrimage because of a great interest in some person, to adore and venerate a particular saint, to do penance perhaps; to go on such a journey with doubts is contrary to the spirit of the pilgrimage itself. A pilgrimage involves travel, but Donne apparently would not even venture next door to find a woman "true and fair." He is so cynical that, even were his plea to be answered and a true woman found, he feels sure that by the time he hears about her she will already have been false to "two or three." Donne's thesis in this poem that a true woman is a most unlikely phenomenon is an example of "hyperbole" (exaggeration). Of course this overstatement is not to be taken literally; it is a device to convey the intensity of the poet's feeling.

What mood has been established by this poem? The answer depends on you. Are you amused, or are you annoyed by the poet's attitude? Whatever your reaction is, I think you will react, for a good poet has always the power of compelling response.

Richard Lovelace (1618–1658) was an English Cavalier poet who fought for the Royalists during the Civil War. "To Lucasta" is a lyric, a short poem that can be sung and that expresses the deeply personal feelings of the singer.

To Lucasta, on Going to the Wars

Tell me not, Sweet, I am unkind,
    That from the nunnery
Of thy chaste breast and quiet mind
    To wars and arms I fly.

True, a new mistress now I chase,
    The first foe in the field;
And with a stronger faith embrace
    A sword, a horse, a shield.

Yet this inconstancy is such
    As thou too shalt adore;
I could not love thee, Dear, so much,
    Loved I not Honour more.

We see that the three stanzas of this poem are written in alternating lines of iambic tetrameter and trimeter and rhyme *a b a b*; this is the stanza form of countless hymns and ballads (and is even called common measure when the lines are in strict iambics). There are, however, some metrical variations in "To Lucasta." The first line, for example, scans

Tell me not, sweet, I am unkind.

Many people regard "To Lucasta" as a perfect poem. What is it that raises this work above the common level? Much of its perfection lies in its compression. In about seventy-five words, values are both stated and implied that no lengthy paraphrase could ever make clearer or more emphatic. How is this achieved?

In the first place, there is a marvelous simplicity; every word counts, really counts. Obviously there has been a lovers' argument:

we guess that Lucasta has been protesting her lover's leaving her to go to war, that with delicate petulance, perhaps, she may have complained of his "unkind" behavior. We catch the placating tone of "Sweet," with which Lucasta is addressed.

Immediately we are drawn into the world of paradox, that is to say of apparent contradiction. We can see clearly what a paradox is if we remember that the United States is the richest country in the world, yet in some regions there is extreme poverty. That this poverty exists would seem to be a contradiction of the assertion that we are the richest country on earth; but the facts remain, despite their apparent contradiction. Irony is inherent in paradox, because there is a disparity between what seems to be and what actually is.

The second line of "To Lucasta" surprises us with the word "nunnery"; it is immediately mystifying. At this point, we must consider the meaning of two words: "denotation" and "connotation." "Denotation" is the literal meaning of a word. The denotation of "nunnery" is, therefore, a residence for nuns. Lovelace, obviously, is not using the word in its literal sense. The connotation of the word is another matter. We define "connotation" as that which we associate with a word—apart from its explicit meaning—by way of feelings, experience, or attitude. Connotation deepens the meaning of a word; it gives it emotional force, sometimes making of it a symbol. What does "nunnery" connote to you? It depends, of course, on your own experience and interests; but to most people there is the suggestion of purity, of quiet, solitude, and order.

It seems contrary to human nature to leave willingly, if not enthusiastically, the "chaste breast and quiet mind" of one's love, for war. To be precise, it is paradoxical; paradox is the language and essence of this poem.

Artfully, in the second stanza, the warrior makes a confession to Lucasta; and this kind of approach, if well-timed, can be disarming. There are other unobtrusive subtleties. Note, for instance, in the second stanza the word "chase"; compare it with "chaste" of the first stanza. The poet is punning. Many of us may sneer indiscriminately at puns. This is unfair, because some puns are very clever indeed. They provide a way of saying much in a little and have at least a double, sometimes even a triple, meaning. Think also of "arms" and "embrace." The poet places these two words in such a way as to draw attention to their derivative relationship.

The paradox of the entire poem hinges on the word "inconstancy" in the last stanza. Inconstancy, or infidelity, is hardly what a woman seeks in her beloved. But this particular "inconstancy," the warrior maintains, is what will prove him worthy of Lucasta's love. The last two lines of the poem, much quoted and among the most eloquent in our language, leave us in no doubt of his integrity:

> I could not love thee, Dear, so much
> Loved I not Honour more.

"The Tyger," a lyric composed in simple trochaic quatrains, is by the mystical English poet and artist, William Blake (1757–1827).

The Tyger

> Tyger! Tyger! burning bright
> In the forests of the night,
> What immortal hand or eye
> Could frame thy fearful symmetry?
>
> In what distant deeps or skies
> Burnt the fire of thine eyes?
> On what wings dare he aspire?
> What the hand dare seize the fire?

And what shoulder & what art,
Could twist the sinews of thy heart?
And when thy heart began to beat,
What dread hand? & what dread feet?

What the hammer? What the chain?
In what furnace was thy brain?
What the anvil? what dread grasp
Dare its deadly terrors clasp?

When the stars threw down their spears,
And water'd heaven with their tears,
Did He smile His work to see?
Did He who made the Lamb make thee?

Tyger! Tyger! burning bright
In the forests of the night,
What immortal hand or eye,
Dare frame thy fearful symmetry?

By addressing the tiger in this poem, Blake is using a device known as "apostrophe" to give life and vigor to his work. In this figure of speech (similar to personification), someone absent or not human is addressed as though he or it were alive and either present or able to answer.

The poet is asking if good and evil emanate from the same source. In his own symbols, did God, who made the lamb (= goodness), also make the tiger (= evil)? The drama is heightened throughout by the frequent use of the words "dare" and "dread," which leap out at the reader (almost like the "tyger" from a thicket). Again and again, they reiterate the profound, unresolved question at the heart of the poem.

Blake himself made, and sometimes engraved, designs in illustration of many works, including his own poems. To give verisimilitude to his works, publishers today traditionally retain the quaint spelling and the ampersands found in contemporary manuscript editions.

Irony

Irony may be defined on its simplest level as the difference between what seems to be and what really is, between what we expect and what actually occurs. If we say, "Nice weather!" when it is raining hard, we have uttered an ironical statement. If we fall into a trap we have set for another, the situation might be termed "ironic justice."

Irony is sometimes amusing. It can be tragic. But whatever emotional response it evokes, irony has a way of striking us sharply, because it contains an element of shock, of surprise, or of disappointment.

Our next poem is heavy with the irony of paradox. It is by the English poet A. E. Housman (1859–1936). About youth and death, it is a lyric in form, with all the neatness and precision of that poetic style at its best.

To an Athlete Dying Young[1]

The time you won your town the race
We chaired you through the market-place;
Man and boy stood cheering by,
And home we brought you shoulder-high.

Today, the road all runners come,
Shoulder-high we bring you home,
And set you at your threshold down,
Townsman of a stiller town.

[1] From "A Shropshire Lad"—authorized edition—from *The Collected Poems of A. E. Housman*. Copyright 1940 by Holt, Rinehart and Winston, Inc.; reprinted by permission of Holt, Rinehart and Winston, Inc.

Smart lad, to slip betimes away
From fields where glory does not stay
And early though the laurel grows
It withers quicker than the rose.

Eyes the shady night has shut
Cannot see the record cut,
And silence sounds no worse than cheers
After earth has stopped the ears:

Now you will not swell the rout
Of lads that wore their honours out,
Runners whom renown outran
And the name died before the man.

So set, before its echoes fade,
The fleet foot on the sill of shade,
And hold to the low lintel up
The still-defended challenge-cup.

And round that early-laureled head
Will flock to gaze the strengthless dead,
And find unwithered on its curls
The garland briefer than a girl's.

In spite of its form, we see that the poem is hardly lyrical
in tone or in content. It is a song, but the poet sings of tragedy.
"Shoulder-high," the triumphantly descriptive final word of the
first stanza, is repeated in the second. But how different is the situation. In a way it is opposite to that of the first, yet the images
connected with victory and death remain almost the same. Compare the "home" of the first stanza with the "home" of the
second.

At no place in this poem is there irony that exceeds the bitterness of

> Smart lad, to slip betimes away.

As though to die were a clever victory over the inevitable malevolence of life! Indeed the runner has won another race; he is first among his competitors to reach the final goal of life—death. In

> Runners whom renown outran
> And the name died before the man

we find the opposite of what we should like to expect.

"To an Athlete Dying Young" gives us an opportunity of examining the symbol as a poetic device. Housman uses it skillfully. In its simplest form, a symbol stands for something different from and usually larger than itself. On highways the symbol + indicates crossroads. In mathematics the figure ∞ signifies infinity. In religion, a cross is the symbol of Christianity, a six-pointed star that of Judaism, the crescent that of Islam. A particularly fascinating use of symbol is afforded by the early Christians, who made the fish the symbol of their belief and, to avoid detection by their persecutors, a password. The Greek word for fish ἰχθύς provides the initial letters of Ἰησοῦς Χριστὸς Θεοῦ υἱὸς Σωτήρ, which means "Jesus, the Christ, the Son of God, and the Savior." In writing, letters and combinations of letters stand for sounds that combine to express ideas and even other symbols. In music, notes symbolize a particular pitch and its duration. Escutcheons tell the origins and rank of a family through symbols. Cattle brands are symbols of ownership. The list is almost endless.

But a word of caution. Symbols are so various and so tenuous that in poetry we sometimes think we find them where they have never existed, or we make them more important than the poet intended them to be. This can lead to a distortion or misrepresentation of the poet's meaning.

Housman's symbols are not obscure; as a matter of fact, they are traditional. The poet contrasts them in such a way that they contribute to the irony of his quoted poem; from the time of the ancient Greeks the laurel has symbolized victory, and the rose has long been a symbol of beauty, especially youthful beauty. Victory and fame, Housman is telling us, are shorter lived even than beauty.

Free Verse

We come now to the "Journey of the Magi," by T. S. Eliot (1888-1965). It is the only poem in this collection written in free verse:

Journey of the Magi[2]

"A cold coming we had of it,
Just the worst time of the year
For a journey, and such a long journey:
The ways deep and the weather sharp,
The very dead of winter."
And the camels galled, sore-footed, refractory,
Lying down in the melting snow.
There were times we regretted
The summer palaces on slopes, the terraces,
And the silken girls bringing sherbet.
Then the camel men cursing and grumbling
And running away, and wanting their liquor and women,
And the night-fires going out, and the lack of shelters,
And the cities hostile and the towns unfriendly
And the villages dirty and charging high prices:

---

[2] From *Collected Poems 1909-1962* by T. S. Eliot. Copyright 1936 by Harcourt, Brace & World, Inc.; © 1963, 1964 by T. S. Eliot; reprinted by permission of the publishers.

A hard time we had of it.
At the end we preferred to travel all night,
Sleeping in snatches,
With the voices singing in our ears, saying
That this was all folly.

Then at dawn we came down to a temperate valley,
Wet, below the snow line, smelling of vegetation;
With a running stream and a water-mill beating the darkness,
And three trees on the low sky,
And an old white horse galloped away in the meadow.
Then we came to a tavern with vine-leaves over the lintel,
Six hands at an open door dicing for pieces of silver,
And feet kicking the empty wine-skins.
But there was no information, and so we continued
And arrived at evening, not a moment too soon
Finding the place; it was (you may say) satisfactory.

All this was a long time ago, I remember,
And I would do it again, but set down
This set down
This: were we led all that way for
Birth or Death? There was a Birth, certainly,
We had evidence and no doubt. I had seen birth and death,
But had thought they were different; this Birth was
Hard and bitter agony for us, like Death, our death.
We returned to our places, these Kingdoms,
But no longer at ease here, in the old dispensation,
With an alien people clutching their gods.
I should be glad of another death.

    Free verse does not follow a regular metrical pattern, nor is
it usually in stanzas. A comparatively recent development, it is a
main element of what could be called the "modern art" of poetry.

Yet abandonment of conventional form does not mean a rejection of rhythm, sound, imagery, and other poetic devices. Even though we cannot fit the whole into a standard metrical pattern, certainly the first part of the "Journey of the Magi" is rhythmical. Balanced phrases joined repeatedly by "and" suggest a steady progression and emphasize the natural rhythm of the camel caravan.

The narrative is in the form of a monologue by one of the Three Wise Men, long after they had followed the star to Bethlehem and had grown old. ("Magi" is the plural of "magus," a priestly philosopher, astrologer, or soothsayer.) As is true of most of Eliot's works, it helps to have background knowledge and some experience in reading poetry. Nevertheless, even if we lack these, we are struck by the immediacy of the lines, their sense of contemporaneity; though we know it all took place so long ago, Eliot makes it seem as though it had happened to us: we share the Magi's experience.

The beginning lines, set in quotation marks, are taken from a Christmas sermon by Lancelot Andrewes (1555–1626), bishop successively of Chichester, Ely, and Winchester. They were, of course, originally written as prose; yet by maintaining their conversational tone, Eliot's adaptation of these lines to verse heightens the reader's sense of being present. Rather than an ecstatic paean on the birth of Christ, we have an objective statement of resignation to a force not quite understood by the Wise Men. The physical aspects of the trip—of no consequence compared with its real significance—stand out in the narrator's mind more clearly than the birth that utterly changed his life and has made him long for death. The clarity with which he recalls superficial details is in direct contrast with his uncertainty about the meaning of his experience. A compelling faith, enough for them to give up a life of ease and position, has driven the Magi on, despite obstructions and delays. Yet this faith is never named; it is only implied.

In the first section of the poem, the imagery is merely descriptive; in the second, the images assume a symbolic function, or a second level of meaning. The narrator continues his description:

> Then at dawn we came down to a temperate valley,
> Wet, below the snow line, smelling of vegetation;
> With a running stream and a water-mill beating the darkness,

—a new day, a new place, a new life, a birth.

But, instantly, in the following line the reader perceives the crosses on Calvary and Christ's death:

> And three trees on the low sky,

The allusion is further enhanced by the "old white horse"—the pale horse, or death, of the Apocalypse, and

> Six hands at an open door dicing for pieces of silver,

recalls in one line the soldiers' casting lots for Christ's raiment and Judas' betrayal for thirty pieces of silver.

The Wise Man must continue living in a physical world that he has rejected by accepting Him who came to transform it. And in this paradoxical and ironic situation, the only hope is that undefined faith that led him on his journey in the first place.

6

Light and Satiric Verse

Most of the poetry in this book is serious in content; it deals with the graver aspects of life. And, although in this last chapter the poems are light and engagingly humorous, even in them much will be found that is serious. Certainly their primary intention is to amuse, but sometimes, beneath an apparently nonsensical surface, a profound idea or feeling is being suggested. Here, the poet achieves his often moving effects by contrast, by a vivacious, if not lusty, use of light and shade.

Of all the facets of the human personality none is so individual as humor. Humor not only varies from person to person, but from society to society, country to country, and era to era. Grief and sorrow, on the other hand, differ little outwardly from one person to another. One either cries or holds back one's tears. Grief tends to dull the imagination, but humor stimulates it.

It is natural that many great poets feel drawn to humor. With variety and wit, they find yet another means of demonstrating their unique view of life.

Satire is a form of criticism with a special purpose—to reform or improve people, ideas, or institutions, by setting them up for ridicule. It is positive criticism, although at times very harsh. The satirist finds humor one of his chief devices because it can serve as sugar-coating to the pill. The following ballade, by E. B. White (b. 1899), is a satire.

The Ballade of Meaty Inversions[1]

"Cold ran the blood of a Finnish farmer"—*Time*

Cold ran the blood of a Finnish farmer,
      Backward the flight of a sentence in *Time*.
Fair was the weather prediction and warmer,
      Thin was the normal American dime.
      Slaked was the typical bucket of lime,
Broken in spirit the average treaty,
      Nobody's any more tired than I'm.
      Poison to me is a sentence too meaty.

Keyed was the skeleton up to his armor
      Fairly ridiculous was the sublime,
Potted the folks in the county of Parmer,
      Ribbed was the beef that was past its prime.
      Fitting the punishment was the crime,
Toasted in cheese was the reached-for sweety,
      Norman as hell was the opera chime:
Poison to me is a sentence too meaty.

Hot was the blaze of the three-alarmer,
      Dated the coffee in every clime,
Princely the sum of the serpent charmer,
      Up was the brontosaur from slime.
      Cool was the air in the cinemime,
Admirable was the naval beatty,[2]
      Long are ballades for all who try 'em:
Poison to me is a sentence too meaty.

[1] From *The Fox of Peapack* by E. B. White. Copyright 1933, 1961 by E. B. White; reprinted with the permission of Harper & Row, Publishers.
[2] British admiral (1871–1936) who won the Battle of Jutland in 1916, one of the hardest-fought battles of World War I.

Envoy

Prince, I regard it as quite a shime,
   Ill lies the land of the thinsy wheaty,
Reasonable is the poet's rhyme:
   Poison to me is a sentence too meaty.

As satires go, this is gentle; but even so it ridicules. The poet pokes good-natured fun not only at the style of the magazine that inspired him, but at advertising, time-worn expressions, the "ballade" form, and finally at his own creation. Some of the allusions in this particular poem may be lost on readers who do not know, for example, that a few years ago the distributors of a certain brand of coffee dated each tin as it was filled, to assure the purchaser of the freshness of the product. By its very nature satire, if it is to achieve its purpose, must be topical.

Edward Lear (1812–1888), an example of whose work is now given, was an English painter and writer best known for his limericks and nonsense verse.

The Nutcrackers and the Sugar-Tongs

I

The Nutcrackers sate by a plate on the table;
   The Sugar-tongs sate by a plate at his side;
And the Nutcrackers said, "Don't you wish we were able
   Along the blue hills and green meadows to ride?
Must we drag on this stupid existence forever,
   So idle and weary, so full of remorse,
While every one else takes his pleasure, and never
   Seems happy unless he is riding a horse?

II

"Don't you think we could ride without being instructed,
    Without any saddle or bridle or spur?
Our legs are so long, and so aptly constructed,
    I'm sure that an accident could not occur.
Let us all of a sudden hop down from the table,
    And hustle downstairs, and each jump on a horse!
Shall we try? Shall we go? Do you think we are able?"
    The Sugar-tongs answered distinctly, "Of course!"

III

So down the long staircase they hopped in a minute;
    The Sugar-tongs snapped, and the Crackers said "Crack!"
The stable was open; the horses were in it:
    Each took out a pony, and jumped on his back.
The Cat in a fright scrambled out of the doorway;
    The Mice tumbled out of a bundle of hay;
The brown and white Rats, and the black ones from Norway,
    Screamed out, "They are taking the horses away!"

IV

The whole of the household was filled with amazement:
    The Cups and the Saucers danced madly about;
The Plates and the Dishes looked out of the casement;
    The Salt-cellar stood on his head with a shout;
The Spoons, with a clatter, looked out of the lattice;
    The Mustard-pot climbed up the gooseberry-pies;
The Soup-ladle peeped through a heap of veal-patties,
    And squeaked with a ladle-like scream of surprise.

V

The Frying-pan said, "It's an awful delusion"
   The Tea-kettle hissed, and grew black in the face;
And they all rushed downstairs in the wildest confusion
   To see the great Nutcracker-Sugar-tong race.
And out of the stable, with screamings and laughter
   (Their ponies were cream-coloured, speckled with brown),
The Nutcrackers first, and the Sugar-tongs after,
   Rode all round the yard, and then all round the town.

VI

They rode through the street, and they rode by the station;
   They galloped away to the beautiful shore;
In silence they rode, and "made no observation,"
   Save this: "We will never go back any more!"
And still you might hear, till they rode out of hearing,
   The Sugar-tongs snap, and the Cracker say "Crack!"
Till, far in the distance their forms disappearing,
   They faded away; and they never came back!

Much great humor has at its core a poignancy, a stinging kind of sadness that is intensified by contrast. If you have ever seen Charlie Chaplin or Harpo Marx or heard *Don Giovanni* or *Till Eulenspiegel*, or watched Cyrano de Bergerac or Falstaff you will recall that under the fun and jesting and gaiety there is sadness.

Even in this preposterous poem, there is a touch of poignancy. True, nutcrackers and sugar tongs are not likely to inspire pathos; yet the mood created is melancholy and even touching, as this ridiculous pair, scorned by equally nonsensical characters, achieve their own personal victory as they "faded away and never came back."

It may seem insensitive to place "Mr. Flood's Party," by Edwin Arlington Robinson (1869–1935), among a group of humorous poems, since dereliction—the subject of the poem—can scarcely be considered laughable. But here again, through humor, the poet creates pathos. He is compassionate, yet his shrewdly humorous wit makes the reader smile.

Mr. Flood's Party[3]

Old Eben Flood, climbing alone one night
Over the hill between the town below
And the forsaken upland hermitage
That held as much as he should ever know
On earth again of home, paused warily.
The road was his with not a native near;
And Eben, having leisure, said aloud,
For no man else in Tilbury Town to hear:

"Well, Mr. Flood, we have the harvest moon
Again, and we may not have many more;
The bird is on the wing, the poet says,
And you and I have said it here before.
Drink to the bird." He raised up to the light
The jug that he had gone so far to fill,
And answered huskily: "Well, Mr. Flood,
Since you propose it, I believe I will."

[3] Reprinted with the permission of The Macmillan Company from *Avon's Harvest* by Edwin Arlington Robinson. Copyright 1921 by Edwin Arlington Robinson, renewed 1949 by Ruth Nivison.

Alone, as if enduring to the end
A valiant armor of scarred hopes outworn,
He stood there in the middle of the road
Like Roland's ghost winding a silent horn.
Below him, in the town among the trees,
Where friends of other days had honored him,
A phantom salutation of the dead
Rang thinly till old Eben's eyes were dim.

Then, as a mother lays her sleeping child
Down tenderly, fearing it may awake,
He set the jug down slowly at his feet
With trembling care, knowing that most things break;
And only when assured that on firm earth
It stood, as the uncertain lives of men
Assuredly did not, he paced away.
And with his hand extended paused again:

"Well, Mr. Flood, we have not met like this
In a long time; and many a change has come
To both of us, I fear, since last it was
We had a drop together. Welcome home!"
Convivially returning with himself,
Again he raised the jug up to the light;
And with an acquiescent quaver said:
"Well, Mr. Flood, if you insist, I might.

"Only a very little, Mr. Flood—
For auld lang syne. No more, sir; that will do."
So, for the time, apparently it did,
And Eben evidently thought so too;
For soon amid the silver loneliness
Of night he lifted up his voice and sang,
Secure, with only two moons listening,
Until the whole harmonious landscape rang—

"For auld lang syne." The weary throat gave out,
The last word wavered; and the song being done,
He raised again the jug regretfully
And shook his head, and was again alone.
There was not much that was ahead of him,
And there was nothing in the town below—
Where strangers would have shut the many doors
That many friends had opened long ago.

Mr. Flood's dialogue with himself, the tender way he sets his
jug upon the earth, "knowing that most things break," his courteous treatment of himself, the phrase "with only two moons listening," with its suggestion of inebriation—all manifest that incon-
gruity which is the basis of much humor. The reference to
Roland and the allusion to *The Rubáiyát* increase the comic in
this poem while intensifying the pathetic. A touching old man,
Mr. Flood evokes both laughter and pity.

The Limerick

The limerick is said to be the only indigenous English verse form.
It was popularized by Edward Lear, and made its first appearance
as an iambic quatrain composed of two trimeter lines followed by
one of tetrameter and concluded with a line of trimeter. As you
see, the rhyme scheme is *a a b a:*

There was a Young Lady whose chin
Resembled the point of a pin;
So she had it made sharp, and purchased a harp,
And played several tunes with her chin.

Since that time it has developed into a five-line iambic stanza
consisting of two consecutive trimeter lines, two dimeter, and
a final trimeter. Here is a modern limerick, by Conrad Aiken
(b. 1889). The rhyme scheme is *a a b b a.*

Said Isolde to Tristan[4]

Said Isolde to Tristan, how curious!
Old Mark is becoming quite furious
    Since we got off that boat
    It's been all Liebestod.
Is it possible Wagner is spurious?

Not suited to serious thought, the limerick is the favorite of humorists and amateur poets. What it lacks in dignity it makes up for in popularity.

You have now concluded an introduction to the techniques of poetry. Perhaps, at this point, you will find it stimulating as well as educational to try writing some poetry yourself—for nothing will make you more appreciative of the poet's art. You need not begin with the most complicated or the most demanding forms of verse; make up a limerick or two, for there is no easier verse to write, and perhaps none more readily enjoyable. If you wish to progress to a more difficult form, write a sonnet. This indeed will be a challenge. It is always possible that in one of you may lie the seeds of that talent which has given the noblest expression to the noblest thoughts of man.

[4] From *A Seizure of Limericks* by Conrad Aiken. © 1963 by Conrad Aiken; reprinted by permission of Holt, Rinehart and Winston, Inc.

Meter

Although most students of poetry use the terms *rhythm* and *meter* interchangeably, they are not the same technically. *Rhythm* encompasses not only what is specifically *meter*, but also pace, tempo, and fluctuations in movement. It is meter, the more or less regular pattern of stressed and unstressed syllables in a poem, that distinguishes verse from prose.

To discover the meter of a particular line we must divide the words into syllables and then hear where the stress, or accent, falls. Those who do not immediately discern the stresses in a line may be aided by tapping out syllables on a hard surface—with your foot, for instance. In words of more than one syllable, only one syllable receives a heavy, or primary, stress; but another syllable in the word can receive a light, or secondary, stress—for example, the primary stress in *caǹ non* becomes secondary in *can non ad́e* and in *can non eér ing.* Monosyllables are accented or not according to their grammatical importance or to the metrical requirements of the line:

> Aňd nońe/ wǐll griéve/ wheň Í/ gŏ forth/ ŏr smíle/
>
> wheň Í/ rĕturń.

The unit of measurement in verse is the *foot*, which is a group of either two or three syllables. Common are the two-

syllable, or dissyllabic, feet, which are the *iambus* ˘ ´ (annóy)
and the *trochee* ´ ˘ (bárgain); and the three-syllable, or trisyllabic, feet, which are the *anapest* ˘ ˘ ´ (intervéne) and the dactyl
´ ˘ ˘ (ínstantly). Less usual, the spondee ´ ´ , the pyrrhic ˘ ˘ ,
and the amphibrach ˘ ´ ˘ , are met occasionally intermixed with
other feet.

The number of feet in a line varies from one to eight. If the
line consists of a single foot, it is called *monometer*; two, *dimeter*; three, *trimeter*; four, *tetrameter*; five, *pentameter*; six,
hexameter; seven, *heptameter*; and eight, *octameter*. Occasionally
at the beginning or ending of a line there is a single accented syllable which counts as an entire foot.

$$\text{Fáre/ yĕ wéel/ mў móth/ ĕr déar}$$

is considered a tetrameter, even though the first foot is deficient.
Likewise

$$\text{Níght ĭs/ dráwĭng/ nígh}$$

is considered a trimeter.

An unaccented syllable added at the end of an iambic or
anapestic lines does not constitute a foot. It is called a feminine
ending. The first five lines of Hamlet's soliloquy, "To be, or
not to be," all have feminine endings.

To scan a line of verse means to determine its meter. As
you have already observed, ˘ indicates unstressed syllables and
´ stressed syllables. Sometimes a slash mark separates feet. Thus

$$\text{Nŏt már/ blĕ, nór/ thĕ gíld/ ĕd món/ ŭménts}$$

is marked to show a line of iambic pentameter.

Over three-fourths of all English verse is iambic. It is the
meter of most long poems and verse plays as well as of sonnets,
ballads, and countless other forms. Although in English the

accent of most words of more than two syllables is recessive—
that is, accented toward the beginning of the word—iambic
is the natural meter of the language because of the frequent
recurrence of unaccented monosyllabic prepositions, articles,
auxiliaries, and conjunctions, which impart an iambic measure
to our speech. Poetry written in iambics seems, therefore, more
natural than that written in other feet.

The trochaic foot, livelier than the iambic, is often used
in poems containing cheerful themes or describing vigorous
action:

> Live thy/ life
> Young and/ old
> Like yon/ oak
> Bright in/ spring,
> Living/ gold.

Anapests and dactyls are not widely used by English
poets, because one stressed to each two unstressed syllables
is not easily afforded by our language. Since it is less natural
than iambic or trochaic verse, the rhythm of trisyllabic measure
is more pronounced than that of dissyllabic and can become
monotonous. For that reason poets writing in anapests or dactyls
frequently interchange feet and add or omit syllables. This
practice is called *substitution* and can produce a rhythm that is
more musical than any that would obtain from a strict adherence
to these particular feet.

The first of the following examples of anapestic tetrameter
is called *pure*, or *symmetrical*, because it contains no substitution:

> Like the leaves/ of the for/ est when sum/ mer is green.

Yet the very first line of the poem:

The Ássyr/ ian came dówn/ like a wólf/ on the fóld

demands that we elide the four syllables of "*As sýr i an*" into three and pronounce it "*As sýr yan*."

The dactyl bears the same relation to the anapest as the trochee does to the iambus. It too is a vigorous meter:

Cánnon to/ ríght of thĕm,

Cánnon to/ léft of thĕm

The following line illustrates substituting spondaic and pyrrhic feet in a line from a work that is iambic:

From thĕ/ Gréat Déep/ to thĕ/ Gréat Déep/ he góes.

There can be, it must be noted, justifiable differences in respect to the scansion of some lines. The following line:

The déw ŏf/ the mórnĭng/ sank chíll ŏn/ my brów.

thus scanned consists of *amphibrachs* and a concluding iambus. We can, however, scan it so that it is dactylic in character:

The/ déw of thĕ/ mórning sank/ chíll on my/ brów.

There is even a third possibility: that is, beginning the line with an iambus so that the remaining feet are anapestic:

The déw/ of the mórn/ ing sank chíll/ on my brów.

It will be seen that the difference among the three is not in stress, but in the way the syllables are grouped.

A Glossary of Terms

ACCENT Emphasis, or stress, placed on a syllable when spoken. Not more than one syllable in an English word receives a heavy, or primary, accent, ´, although another syllable in the same word may be lightly stressed, or receive a secondary accent, ` —e.g., mán da tò ry.

ALEXANDRINE A twelve-syllable (hexameter) iambic line.

> A needless alexandrine ends the song
> Thăt lĭke/ ă woúnd/ ĕd snáke,/ drágs ĭts/
> slŏw léngth/ ălóng
>
> —Pope

ALLEGORY As a literary form, it is a narrative in which events or characters or both are symbolic, such as Bunyan's *Pilgrim's Progress*. As a figure of speech, an allegory is an extended simile or metaphor making a point-by-point comparison—e.g., Longfellow's sonnet "Nature."

ALLITERATION The repetition of identical consonant sounds.

> Whereat, with blade, with bloody, blameful blade
> He bravely broached his boiling, bloody breast.
>
> —Shakespeare

AMPHIBRACH A trisyllabic foot consisting of an unstressed syllable followed by one stressed and one unstressed syllable ˘ ´ ˘

ANAPEST A trisyllabic foot consisting of two unstressed syllables followed by one stressed syllable.

130

For the moon never beams without bringing me dreams
  of the beautiful Annabel Lee;
And the stars never rise but I feel the bright eyes
  Of the beautiful Annabel Lee.

—Poe

APOSTROPHE A figure of speech in which someone absent or a thing or an idea is addressed as though present and able to respond.

> Hence, loathed Melancholy
>   Of Cerberus and blackest Midnight born,
> In Stygian cave forlorn,
>   'Mongst horrid shapes, and shrieks, and
>   sights unholy,
> Find out some uncouth cell. . . .

—Milton

BALLADE Preferably three eight-line stanzas of iambic or anapestic tetrameter and an envoy of four lines. The last line of the opening stanza concludes the remaining two and the envoy. The stanzas rhyme *a b a b b c b c*, and the envoy *b b c c*.

BALLAD STANZA Four alternating lines of iambic tetrameter and trimeter, rhyming *a b c b*.

BLANK VERSE Any unrhyming verse, but usually iambic pentameter—e.g., Milton's *Paradise Lost*, most of the verse in Shakespeare's plays, etc.

CAESURA A pause, usually grammatical, within a line. It is marked ✓✓.

> Winds take a pensive tone, ✓✓ and stars a tender fire,
> And visions rise, ✓✓ and change, ✓✓ that kill me with desire.

—Emily Brontë

COMMON MEASURE   Often abbreviated "C.M." An iambic quatrain of alternating tetrameter and trimeter, rhyming *a b c b* or *a b a b*. Its strict adherence to iambics distinguishes it from the ballad stanza, in which frequent metrical variations occur.

> While shep/ herds watched/ their flocks/ by night,
>   All seat/ ed on/ the ground,
> The an/ gel of/ the Lord/ came down,
>   And glo/ ry shone/ around.
>
> —Tate

CONCEIT   An elaborate image—e.g., "The Pulley" by George Herbert.

CONNOTATION   Meanings, attitudes, and emotions associated with a word.

COUPLET, or DISTICH   Two lines of rhyming verse.

> Men, my brothers, men the workers, ever reaping something new;
> That which they have done but earnest of the things that they
>   shall do.
>
> —Tennyson

The heroic couplet is written in iambic pentameter and contains a complete thought.

> Is there no bright reversion in the sky
> For those who greatly think, or bravely die?
>
> —Pope

DACTYL   A trisyllabic foot of one stressed syllable followed by two unstressed syllables.

> Make no deep/ scrutiny
> Into her/ mutiny.
>
> —Hood

DENOTATION Meaning or definition.

DIMETER A line consisting of two feet.

$$\text{Rích thĕ/ tréasŭre,}$$
$$\text{Swéet thĕ/ pléasŭre.}$$

—Dryden

DISSYLLABIC FOOT A foot of two syllables—the iambus, trochee, spondee, and pyrrhic.

DRAMATIC MONOLOGUE A poem in which a story is related by a single person speaking to one or more persons, but in such a way as to give the impression that there is more than one speaker or participant in the action narrated.

ELEGY A meditative poem or a lament for the dead—e.g., "A Slumber Did My Spirit Seal" by Wordsworth.

ENGLISH SONNET, or SHAKESPEAREAN SONNET Fourteen lines of iambic pentameter divided into three quatrains and a concluding couplet, rhyming *a b a b, c d c d, e f e f, g g*. Usually each quatrain expresses in figurative language an aspect of the thought of the poem, which is summed up in the concluding couplet.

ENJAMBMENT The continuation of the sense of one line to the next without any grammatical pause. Frequently called a run-on line.

ENVOY, or ENVOI A stanza at the end of a ballade, half the length of the ballade stanza. It forms an emphatic restatement of the sentiment expressed in the poem.

EPIC A long dignified rhythmic narrative of a momentous theme or action involving heroic characters and, frequently, super-natural agencies under the control of a sovereign destiny.

EPIGRAM A short pithy poem or saying of two or four lines, containing a neatly expressed thought, often satirical.

EPITAPH An inscription intended for a tombstone—e.g., the concluding three quatrains of Gray's "Elegy Written in a Country Churchyard."

EPITHET A descriptive phrase, a noun, or an adjective, used with a name or in place of it—e.g., Eric the Red, the Snow-Haired Zal, Mack the Knife.

EYE RHYME Rhymes that agree in spelling, but not in sound—e.g., through/rough; love/move.

FEMININE ENDING An extra unstressed syllable at the end of a line.

To be/, or not/ to be/ that is/ the ques/ tion:

Whether/ 'tis no/ bler in/ the mind/ to suf/ fer . . .

—Shakespeare

FEMININE RHYME A rhyme of two syllables, with the second unstressed—e.g., grazes/hazes; Tophet/prophet.

FIGURATIVE LANGUAGE Words used in a new and unliteral sense. The most common figures are the simile, metaphor, metonymy, synecdoche, personification, allegory, hyperbole, litotes, and apostrophe (see separate listings).

FOOT The metrical unit consisting of either two or three syllables. Unstressed syllables are marked ˘ ; and stressed ´ .

FORM Prescribed meter, length of lines, and rhyme scheme which constitute a particular organization—e.g., the sonnet, the ballad, etc.

FREE VERSE Poetry that does not follow a prescribed form, but rather is characterized by irregularity in the length of lines and the lack of a regular metrical pattern and rhyme.

GENRE   The form or type of literary work—e.g., novel, play, epic, etc.

HEPTAMETER   A line consisting of seven feet.

"It's bit/ ter cóld,/ it's bit/ter cold,"/ the Cól/

or-Ser/ geant said.

—Kipling

HEXAMETER   A line consisting of six feet.

Hóly,/ Hóly,/ Hóly,/ All the/ saints a/ dore thee.

—Heber

HYPERBOLE   A figure of speech that exaggerates for effect.

Continuous as the stars that shine
And twinkle on the Milky Way,
They stretch'd in never-ending line
Along the margin of a bay:
Ten thousand saw I at a glance,
Tossing their heads in sprightly dance.

—Wordsworth

IAMBUS   A dissyllabic foot consisting of an unstressed syllable followed by a stressed syllable.

When Í/ consíd/ er hów/ my líght/ is spént.

—Milton

IMAGE   A sense perception reproduced in the mind.

INCREMENTAL REPETITION   A device of the ballad which repeats what has been said before while advancing the action.

O, Where hae ye been, Lord Randal, my son?
O, Where hae ye been, my handsome young man?—
I hae been to the wild wood; mother, make my bed soon,
For I'm weary wi' hunting, and fain wald lie down.

Where gat ye your dinner, Lord Randal, my son?
Where gat ye your dinner, my handsome young man?
I dined wi' my true-love; mother, make my bed soon,
For I'm weary wi' hunting, and fain wald lie down.

—Anonymous

INTERNAL RHYME   Words rhyming within a line, or one within
the line rhyming with the word at the end of the line.

To dance to flutes, to dance to lutes
Is delicate and rare.

—Wilde

IRONY   That which results when there occurs the opposite of
what was meant, intended, or expected.

ITALIAN SONNET, or PETRARCHAN SONNET   Fourteen lines of iambic
pentameter rhyming in the octave *a b b a a b b a*, and in the
sestet *c d c d c d* (or some variation thereof). The octave usually
expresses in figurative language what is restated in direct language
in the sestet.

LIMERICK   Either an iambic quatrain of two trimeter lines, followed by one of tetrameter and concluded with one of trimeter,
rhyming *a a b a;* or a five-line stanza of two iambic trimeter
lines, followed by two dimeter and a final trimeter rhyming
a a b b a.

LITOTES   A figure of speech in which an affirmation is made
through the negative of its contrary.

Not unworthy, not inglorious son.

—Arnold

LONG METER   Commonly abbreviated "L.M." A stanza of four
lines of iambic tetrameter, rhyming *a b a b* or *a b c b*.

Strŏng Són/ ŏf Gŏd/ ĭmmór/ tăl lóve,
Whŏm wé/ thăt háve/ nŏt séen/ thў fáce,
Bĕliév/ ĭng whére/ wĕ cán/ nŏt próve,
Bў fáith/ ănd fáith/ ălóne/ ĕmbráce.

—Tennyson

LYRIC   A poem that expresses emotion and is intended to be
sung.

MASCULINE ENDING   A line ending on a stressed syllable.

With rocks/ and stones/ and trees

—Wordsworth

MASCULINE RHYME   Words that rhyme on a final stressed syllable—e.g., cat/rat; acquaint/complaint.

MEASURE   See METER

METAPHOR   An implied or assumed comparison.

The Wine of Life keeps oozing drop by drop

—FitzGerald

METER or MEASURE   The more or less regular pattern of stressed
and unstressed syllables in verse.

METONYMY   A figure of speech that substitutes a word that re-
lates to or suggests the person, place, idea, or thing to be named.

Unless the kettle boiling be,
Filling the teapot spoils the tea.

—Anonymous

MILTONIC SONNET   The rhyme scheme of the Italian sonnet, but without the customary break in sense at the conclusion of the octave.

MIXED METAPHOR   A figurative expression in which the two or more metaphors employed are so opposed or incongruous that they tend to cancel each other out.

> Footprints on the sands of time.
>
> —Longfellow

(Presumably "sands" refers to an hourglass; but even if the poet has the seashore alone in mind, the comparison is inept because nothing shifts and obliterates all traces sooner than does sand.)

MONOMETER   A line consisting of a single foot.

> Thus I
> Pass by
> And die
> As one
> Unknown
> And gone.
>
> —Herrick

MOOD   The emotional atmosphere created by a work of art.

OCTAVE   An eight-line unit of verse.

ODE   An apostrophe of elaborate design and usually vigorous in tone—e.g., "A Song for St. Cecilia's Day, 1687" by Dryden.

ONOMATOPOEIA   A device of sound in which the meaning of a word is suggested by its sound.

> Like the whizz of my crossbow.
>
> —Coleridge

OTTAVA RIMA   An eight-line stanza rhyming *a b a b a b c c*—such as in certain stanzas of *Don Juan* by Byron.

PARADOX   An apparent contradiction, but nonetheless true.

> Water, water, everywhere
> And all the boards did shrink;
> Water, water, everywhere
> Nor any drop to drink.
>
> —Coleridge

PARODY   A device of satire. The exaggeration or imitation of a particular style to create a humorous effect.

PENTAMETER   A line consisting of five feet.

> Shall Í/ compáre/ thee to/ a sum/ mer's day?
>
> —Shakespeare

PERSONIFICATION   A figure of speech in which an animal, thing, or idea is given the characteristics of a human being.

> April, April,
> Laugh thy girlish laughter;
> Then the minute after,
> Weep thy girlish tears!
>
> —Watson

PETRARCHAN SONNET   See ITALIAN SONNET.

PYRRHIC   A foot consisting of two unstressed syllables.

> From the/ Great Deep/ to the/ Great Deep/ he goes.
>
> —Tennyson

QUATRAIN   A four-line unit of verse.

RECESSIVE STRESS   The accent is at the beginning of the word.

RHYME The repetition of similar sounds occurring at determined, or regular, intervals.

RHYME ROYAL A rhyme scheme of *a b a b b c c*—e.g., Chaucer's "Lenvoy de Chaucer à Scogan," Spenser's "Hymne of Heavenly Beautie."

RHYTHM Although sometimes used to signify meter, it includes tempo and the natural fluctuations of movement.

SCANSION The indication of meter. The marks used are ˊ for a stressed syllable; ˘ for an unstressed syllable; / between feet; // at a caesura.

SESTET A six-line unit of verse.

SHAKESPEAREAN SONNET See ENGLISH SONNET.

SHORT METER Commonly abbreviated "S.M." An iambic quatrain in which the first two lines are trimeter, the third is a tetrameter, and the fourth a trimeter. It rhymes either *a b a b* or *a b c b*.

> Blĕst áre/ thĕ púre/ ĭn héart,
> Fŏr théy/ shăll sée/ ŏur Gód.
> Thĕ séc/ rĕt óf/ thĕ Lórd/ ĭs théirs;
> Thĕir sóul/ ĭs Chríst's/ ăbóde.
>
> —Keble

SIMILE A comparison introduced usually by the words "like" or "as."

> A noise like of a hidden brook
> In the leafy month of June
> That to the sleeping woods all night
> Singeth a quiet tune.
>
> —Coleridge

SPENSERIAN SONNET   A variation of the English sonnet. Its rhyme scheme is *a b a b b c b c c d c d e e*—e.g., Spenser's "Amoretti."

SPENSERIAN STANZA   Eight lines of iambic pentameter and a concluding line of iambic hexameter (Alexandrine), rhyming *a b a b b c b c c*. It is the stanza form of Spenser's *Faerie Queene.*

SPONDEE   A foot consisting of two stressed syllables.

Slow spon/ dee stalks,/ strong foot.

—Pope

STANZA   Lines grouped in a pattern which is usually repeated throughout the poem. The distinguishing characteristics of the stanza are the number of lines, the number of feet in each line, and the rhyme scheme.

STRESS   The emphasis or weight given to syllables.

SUBSTITUTION   Replacing an expected foot in a line with one of another meter.

Keen, fit/ ful gusts/ are whis/ pering here/ and there
Among/ the bush/ es half/ leafless/ and dry;
The stars/ look ver/ y cold/ about/ the sky,

And I/ have man/ y miles/ on foot/ to fare,
Yet feel/ I lit/ tle of/ the cool/ bleak air,
Or of/ the dead/ leaves rust/ ling drear/ ily.

—Keats

SYMBOL   That which stands for something other than itself.

SYNECDOCHE   A figure of speech in which the part stands for the whole.

The western wave was all a-flame.

—Coleridge

TERCET   A three-line unit of verse.

TERZA RIMA   A series of tercets rhyming *a b a, b c b, c d c, d e d,* etc.—such as Shelley's "Ode to the West Wind."

TETRAMETER   A line consisting of four feet.

> This lit/ tle vault,/ this nar/ row room,
> Of Love/ and Beau/ ty is/ the tomb;
>
>   —Carew

TONE   The author's attitude as expressed in his work.

TRIMETER   A line consisting of three feet.

> The mon/ arch saw/ and shook,
>   And bade/ no more/ rejoice;
> All blood/ less waxed/ his look,
>   And trem/ ulous/ his voice.
>
>   —Byron

TRIPLET   A group of three lines which rhyme *a a a.*

> Why I tie about thy wrist,
> Julia, this my silken twist;
> For what other reason is't
> But to show thee how, in part,
> Thou my pretty captive art?
> But thy bond-slave in my heart:
>
>   —Herrick

TRISYLLABIC FOOT   A metrical unit consisting of three syllables— the anapest, dactyl, and amphibrach.

TROCHEE   A foot consisting of a stressed syllable followed by an unstressed syllable.

'Tis the/ place, and/ all a/ round it/ as of/ old, the/
curlews/ call.

—Tennyson

VERSE The term refers either to a single line of poetry or to metrical poetry in general. It should not be confused with a stanza.

VILLANELLE A poem of nineteen lines with two rhymes. It is divided into five tercets rhyming *a b a*, with a concluding quatrain rhyming *a b a a*. The first line is repeated at the end of the second, fourth, and sixth tercets, while the third is repeated at the end of the third and fifth tercets and at the end of the concluding quatrain—e.g., Dylan Thomas' "Do Not Go Gentle into That Good Night."

Biographies

CONRAD POTTER AIKEN (b. *1889*)
This American poet, novelist, and short-story writer wrote his
first poem at the age of nine. Educated at Middlesex and Harvard,
Aiken numbered among his university classmates T. S. Eliot,
Van Wyck Brooks, Heywood Broun, and Robert Benchley.
Early in his literary career he associated himself with a group of
poets known as the Imagists. In 1929, he won the Pulitzer Prize
for Poetry for his *Selected Poems*. He now lives in Brewster,
Massachusetts.

MATTHEW ARNOLD (*1822–1888*)
This English poet and critic was the son of Dr. Thomas Arnold,
the famous headmaster of Rugby School. Matthew Arnold himself had a distinguished academic career, achieving one of the
highest distinctions at Oxford, when in 1845 he was made a
Fellow of Oriel College. For a while he taught classics at Rugby,
and in 1857 he returned to Oxford as Professor of Poetry. His
prose works reached prominence with his *Essays in Criticism*.
From 1851 to 1886 he was an inspector of schools, during which
time he attempted to secure the improvement of education in
England. He was a vigorous man whose manner belied the intel-
lectual uncertainty found in much of his poetry.

WILLIAM BLAKE (*1757–1827*)

Apprenticed at an early age to a London engraver, Blake had no formal education. His early training, however, later enabled him to engrave and illustrate many of his own works besides those of Young, Blair, and Graves. Today he is as much admired for his colorful engravings as for his writings. Of a mystical and strange turn of mind, Blake's writing relied heavily on symbols; he created a complex mythology of his own to explain the universe and the problems of good and evil. None of this, however, prevented his having a deep interest in the social problems of his age.

ROBERT BROWNING (*1812–1889*)

This English poet, the son of a clerk in the Bank of England, was privately educated and traveled extensively, chiefly in Italy. In 1846 he married Elizabeth Barrett, whose reputation as a poet at the time far exceeded that of her husband. Later, however, Browning enjoyed such a vogue that societies were organized for the purpose of studying his works. A few of these groups still exist.

SAMUEL TAYLOR COLERIDGE (*1772–1834*)

The son of an English country parson, Coleridge received his schooling at Christ's Hospital in London. In 1791 he entered Cambridge University, but he became what is today called a "drop-out." After a brief period in the army, Coleridge traveled somewhat aimlessly for long periods of time and led a thoroughly undisciplined existence. He was well acquainted with many of the literary figures of the period—Charles Lamb, Robert Southey (who became his brother-in-law), Wordsworth, Hazlitt, Carlyle, and Byron. Despite the perfection of his literary works Coleridge's personal life was not exemplary: he forsook his family; drugs and excessive self-indulgence ruined his health. At the end of his life he was totally dependent upon others and wrote practically nothing. Nevertheless, his work had a great influence on later generations, for in addition to his poetic achievements, he was a philosopher and literary critic of distinction.

JOHN DONNE (1572–1631)

The son of a London hardware dealer, Donne died in that city while Dean of St. Paul's, a cathedral of the Anglican Church. In his early life he was a Roman Catholic. He took Anglican orders in 1615, only sixteen years before his death. In the seventeenth century, a period noted for its sermons, his are among the best. As Dean of St. Paul's he often preached before King Charles I. Donne's life is divided neatly into two periods easily discernible from his writings. The first, up until the time he went into the Church, was characterized by wit and cynicism; the second by piety and reflection. Donne was educated both at Oxford and Cambridge. He eloped with Anne More, whose death a few years later is said to have deeply affected him.

T(HOMAS) S(TEARNS) ELIOT (1888–1965)

Born in St. Louis, Missouri, T. S. Eliot was educated at Harvard, and later at the Sorbonne, and at Oxford. He lived most of his adult life in England, eventually becoming a British subject and, as he described it, an "Anglo-Catholic." The ultimate significance of his contribution to the literature of his age has yet to be measured; but no modern poet is better known, although the quantity of his work is comparatively small. He spoke for the post-World War I generations and has profoundly influenced poetry and criticism since he first began to appear in print. His plays—especially *Murder in the Cathedral*—have won for him a respected place among modern playwrights. In 1948 Mr. Eliot won the Nobel Prize for Literature.

ROBERT (LEE) FROST (*1875–1963*)

Although born in San Francisco, Frost's associations were entirely with New England—his paternal ancestry, his upbringing, and formal education. It is as the spokesman of New Englanders north of Boston that he chiefly is known. Four times awarded the Pulitzer Prize, in his last years he became the unofficial poet laureate of the United States. His formal education was limited, but Frost became poet in residence both at Amherst College and the University of Michigan, and Emerson Professor of Poetry at Harvard. He lectured extensively at colleges and universities throughout the United States.

A(LFRED) E(DWARD) HOUSMAN (*1859–1936*)

A great classical scholar as well as a poet, Housman was reserved and melancholy in manner. Eventually he became something of a recluse. He was educated at Bromsgrove School and at St. John's College, Oxford. In 1882 he passed a civil service examination and worked in the Patent Office as a higher division clerk until 1892, when he was appointed to University College, London. He then began his teaching career. In 1911 he left University College to become Professor of Latin at Trinity College, Cambridge, a post he held until his death twenty-five years later. From all appearances his life was an uneventful one devoted to quiet scholarly pursuit and the writing of lyrics, the most famous collection of which is entitled *A Shropshire Lad*.

JOHN KEATS (*1795–1821*)

As a young man Keats was apprenticed to a London apothecary and studied to become a surgeon. He never practiced, however, because he wished to write. His early works were harshly criticized (particularly *Endymion*), but by the time he was twenty-four he had won recognition for his great odes—"On a Grecian Urn," "To a Nightingale," and "To Autumn." Seriously ill with tuberculosis, Keats sailed to Italy in 1820 and died in Rome the next year.

RUDYARD KIPLING (*1865–1936*)
This English poet, novelist, and short-story writer, and author of children's books was born in India, where he was engaged in journalistic work from 1882 to 1889. Many of his works deal with the country of his birth, and he is frequently thought of as the spokesman of British imperialism. The recent pejorative connotation of "imperialism" has unfairly militated against the works of this serious and accomplished writer.

EDWARD LEAR (*1812–1888*)
This English poet, painter, and humorist is noted for his *Book of Nonsense*, which he wrote for the grandchildren of his patron, the Earl of Derby. In it he popularized the limerick, which is said to be the only indigenous English verse form.

RICHARD LOVELACE (*1618–1658*)
Educated at Charterhouse and Oxford, this talented and handsome poet and soldier was born to great wealth. During the English Civil War he was on the side of the Royalists and was thrown into prison by order of the House of Commons in 1642. Three years later he rejoined Charles I. It was erroneously reported that he was killed, whereupon his fiancée, "Lucasta," married another man. He was again imprisoned for political reasons, and during this period wrote odes and sonnets of incomparable beauty. He died some time after in extreme poverty.

JOHN (GILLESPIE) MAGEE, Jr. (*1922–1941*)
At the age of nineteen Magee, a Canadian, was killed in battle during the Second World War while serving with the R.A.F. Before entering the service he attended school in the United States.

EDNA ST. VINCENT MILLAY (*1892–1950*)
This American poetess was born in Rockland, Maine, and educated at Vassar. After leaving college, Miss Millay lived in Greenwich Village, which at the time was the residence of many serious writers and artists. In 1922 she won the Pulitzer Prize for Poetry. In 1927 her *King's Henchman* provided the book for an opera composed by Deems Taylor and received great acclaim. Miss Millay was a spokesman for the '30's and '40's. She was actively interested in social and political causes; as she grew older and the world became her concern, her poetry lost its original personal nature. At the time of her death in 1950 she was living alone in a remote house near Austerlitz, New York, where she had lived since her marriage in 1923.

EDGAR ALLAN POE (*1809–1849*)
Born in Boston, Massachusetts, Poe was educated first in England, then briefly at the University of Virginia, and finally at the United States Military Academy in West Point, from which he was dismissed in 1831. His first literary work was not successful, and he turned to journalism. As editor of various periodicals, he was given the opportunity to publish his own works. The first to bring him wide popularity was "The Raven," written only four years before his death. Besides his poems and short stories, Poe wrote much literary criticism. Although widely read in his native country, the works of Poe have always been more highly esteemed abroad than here.

EDWIN ARLINGTON ROBINSON (*1869–1935*)
Edwin Arlington Robinson was born in the village of Head Tide, Maine, but at the age of six he and his family moved to Gardiner, Maine—the "Tilbury Town" of his poems. He was a precocious child and began writing verse at eleven. He attended Harvard, but his father's death and reverses in the family fortune caused him to

withdraw before graduation and to remain in Gardiner until his mother's death three years later. He then moved to New York, where Theodore Roosevelt became interested in him and offered him a post in the New York Custom House. Robinson accepted, resigning in 1910 because the position did not leave him time to write poetry. He next went to the MacDowell Colony in Peterborough, New Hampshire—a community established for writers and musicians—and remained there, except for brief periods, for the rest of his life. One of his most distinguished works, which was to establish his reputation, was *The Man against the Sky*, published in 1916. In 1921, his *Collected Poems* won the Pulitzer Prize.

WILLIAM SHAKESPEARE (*1564–1616*)

In 1964 the world celebrated the four-hundredth anniversary of the birth of the greatest writer in the English language. During his lifetime he wrote and produced some thirty-seven or -eight plays; in addition he wrote over one hundred fifty sonnets besides other poems and songs. During his own lifetime Shakespeare was much admired both as a playwright and an actor. Since that time, except during a period of Puritan disapproval of drama in the seventeenth century, Shakespeare's works have continued to grow in popularity, until today there is probably no playwright whose works are more frequently performed.

ALFRED, LORD TENNYSON (*1809–1892*)

Appointed Poet Laureate to succeed William Wordsworth in 1850, Tennyson is one of the most representative English poets of the nineteenth century. His first poem was written when he was very young, upon occasion of his grandmother's death, on the strength of which he was paid a certain sum by his grandfather not to write any more! A few years later, at the age of twelve, he wrote a long work in imitation of Sir Walter Scott, and this time was greatly encouraged to continue writing. While at Trinity

College, Cambridge, the poet met Arthur Henry Hallam, with whom he went to Spain to aid revolutionists of the time. Later Hallam's death inspired Tennyson's *In Memoriam*, one of his greatest works. Tennyson was a man of personal charm and keen intellect as well as poetic ability; that circumstance no doubt accounts for the extraordinary number of friends he is said to have had. His last volume of verse, *The Death of Oenone*, was published the year of his death, when he was eighty-three, and contains the same qualities and strength of intellect shown in his earlier verse. He was created a baron by Queen Victoria in honor of his poetic achievements.

E(LWYN) B(ROOKS) WHITE (b. *1899*)
This American essayist, poet, and author of books for children, is noted for his contributions to the "Talk of the Town" in the *New Yorker*. His *Charlotte's Web* and *Stuart Little* are nearly as well known to children as are *Alice in Wonderland* and *Winnie the Pooh*. The popularity of his *One Man's Meat* and *Points of My Compass*, to name but two of his collections of essays, is proof that this literary form when expertly handled is still greatly admired. Mr. White was born in Mt. Vernon, New York, and educated at Cornell University. He now lives in Maine.

WILLIAM WORDSWORTH (*1770–1850*)
Wordsworth was educated at St. John's College, Cambridge, where he did not distinguish himself as a student. After leaving the university he went on a walking tour in France, the Alps, and Italy. While in Europe he was considerably influenced by the revolutionary movement which was then fomenting. His later writings, however, show that he abandoned the liberalism he had once embraced so enthusiastically. Having been given the position of commissioner of stamps and taxes for the county of Westmorland, Wordsworth was provided with a modest income that

permitted him more leisure to write. In 1843 he succeeded Southey as Poet Laureate. His frequent travels inspired much of his writing. Like Coleridge, Wordsworth was well acquainted with the literary personages of his time.

Index of Authors

Index of Titles

Index of First Lines